Modern Writers

The 'Modern Writers' series

The following are titles in this series of short guides to contemporary international writers:

Alan Bold

Thom Gunn
and Ted Hughes

Oliver & Boyd
Edinburgh

GUNN & HUGHES

Oliver & Boyd

Croythorn House
23 Ravelston Terrace
Edinburgh EH4 3TJ
A Division of Longman Group Ltd.

ISBN 0 05 002855 3 Cased
0 05 002854 5 Paperback

Filmset in Hong Kong by
T.P. Graphic Arts Services
Printed in Hong Kong by
Dai Nippon Printing Co. (H.K.) Ltd.

Contents

To Thom & Ted

There were once two poets called Thom and Ted
Thom spent a lot of time in his bed
Willing the action that worried his head
Feeling no muscle in what men said
   Yet said a lot.

There were once two poets called Ted and Thom
Ted walked the moors the hour before dawn
Hoped mammoths would trample all over the lawn
Saw nothing in brain but a lack of brawn
   Yet thought a lot.

One walked the streets attired in leather
One stalked alone against the weather
Both pondered on the past and whether
Men were alone or lumped together
   As they'd been taught.

And there was sadness behind each smile
As they searched in their domicile
As they hunted all the while
Till they tracked down a searching style
   For what they'd caught.

Alan Bold

Acknowledgements

I would like to thank, first of all, Thom Gunn and Ted Hughes for their co-operation. Throughout the writing of the book I found them both helpful and entertaining correspondents: they made a pleasant task thoroughly enjoyable. Ted Hughes's sister, Olwyn, was most kind to me; and the poet's father, Bill, was a splendid host when I visited him at his Heptonstall home. I am much obliged to my friends Stewart and Kate Crehan of Old Glossop for putting up with me and my family while I completed the book; and to Rosemary Goad of Faber & Faber for all her practical help. For permission to quote copyright material acknowledgements are due to Faber & Faber for quotations from *The Sense of Movement*, *Fighting Terms* and *Touch*; to Faber & Faber and Farrar Straus & Giroux Inc. for quotations from *Moly* and *My Sad Captains* (copyright © 1961, 1971, 1973 by Thom Gunn); to Faber & Faber and Harper & Row for quotations from *Crow* (copyright © 1971 by Ted Hughes), *Wodwo* (copyright © 1967 by Ted Hughes) and *Lupercal* (copyright © 1960 by Ted Hughes); to Faber & Faber and The Bobbs-Merrill Company Inc. for the quotation from *Meet My Folks* (copyright © 1961, 1973 by Ted Hughes); to Faber & Faber and The Viking Press Inc. for the quotation from *The Earth Owl and Other Moon People* (to be published in the United States by Viking Press under the title *Moon Whales and Other Poems* in 1976); to Thom Gunn for the quotations from *Songbook, To the Air* and *Mandrakes*; and to Miss Olwyn Hughes for the quotations from *Spring Summer Autumn Winter* and *Recklings* by Ted Hughes.

Acknowledgements

1   Ted Gunn

In the 1950s it seemed as if a collective poet was about to be let loose on the fragile literary public: Ted Gunn. Amidst a barely concealed fascination with toughness and violence the critics hatched Ted Gunn who was credited with enough explosive power to dynamite his way through brains accustomed only to passive reflection. Ted Gunn was young and tough and vigorous and aggressively masculine and darkly sinister—Nazi or Nietszchean if not both. Ted Gunn creaked about in leather in pursuit of predatory animals. Ted Gunn was alive. But Ted Gunn was a critical and journalistic invention. The critics were using poetry to illustrate trends rather than considering it on its own terms. However, there is seldom critical smoke without some creative fire.

Thom Gunn and Ted Hughes had some things in common. Their names were monosyllabic and, more significantly, alphabetically consecutive so that they were seldom apart in alphabetically arranged anthologies. Chronologically they were close, too: Gunn was born in 1929, Hughes in 1930. Before going up to Trinity College, Cambridge, to read English Gunn did two years National Service in the army. Before going up to Pembroke College, Cambridge, to read English Hughes did two years National Service in the RAF. They are both published in the UK by Faber and Faber who celebrated the popular interest in the pair by bringing out a paperback, *Selected Poems by Thom Gunn and Ted Hughes*, in May 1962. The enormous sales of this two-man anthology indicate that the poetry-reading public certainly bought the package.

What that public also bought was the fallacy that the two poets were poets of violence. This is the image that the critics kept hammering home. It was said of Gunn, 'he is a tough thinker writing for intellectual toughs like himself'[1] and of Hughes, 'He

---

1 *The Times Educational Supplement*, 3 August 1956, p. 995.

is a bruiser who pummels his readers with the harshest, most solid words in order to batter them into submission'.[2] Another writer has said, typically:

> There are no moral overtones to mitigate the violence in either Thom Gunn, one of whose characters repeats 'I regret nothing', or in Ted Hughes, for whose creatures the hawk speaks when it says, 'No arguments assert my right'.[3]

So the convenient classification of Gunn and Hughes is that of the terrible twins of violence in poetry. A reading of the work of the two poets will, however, reveal that Gunn's poetry centres around his personal search for an identity while Hughes's work stands in awe of the elements of nature. These are honest concerns, concerns that can sustain poetry, but they are not conspicuously violent. Compared with the work of Shakespeare or the Jacobean dramatists, the work of Gunn and Hughes seems positively pacific. Yet in the rarefied world of literary criticism, poems about motor cyclists and predatory birds seem excessively violent. When it is remembered that most critics could not punch their way out of a paperback it is not so surprising that they experience a shiver of menace when confronted by the work of poets who respond to the spectacle of energy. But in a world of permanently imminent war Thom Gunn and Ted Hughes cannot be accused of wallowing in violence.

It is as well to clear up this subject at the outset as both poets have felt it to be a red herring deflecting attention away from their poetry. Hughes has said 'My poems are not about violence but vitality. Animals are not violent, they're so much more completely controlled than men. So much more adapted to their environment'.[4] He has also said:

> When my Aunt calls my verse 'horrible and violent' I know what she means.... What she has is an idea of

2 John Press, *Rule and Energy*, London (Oxford University Press) 1963, p. 182.
3 H.G. Earnshaw, *Modern Writers*, Edinburgh and London (W. & R. Chambers) 1968, p. 259.
4 *The Guardian*, 23 March 1965, p. 9.

what poetry ought to be...a very vague idea, since it's based on an almost total ignorance of what poetry has been written....In a sense, critics who find my poetry violent are in her world, and they are safeguarding her way of life. So to define their use of the word violence any further, you have to work out just why her way of life should find the behaviour of a hawk 'horrible' or any reference to violent death 'disgusting'....If one were to answer that exam question: Who are the poets of violence? you wouldn't get very far if you began with Thom Gunn...and not merely because his subject is far more surely gentleness.[5]

Hughes's observation on Gunn's work is a fair one for Gunn, by his upbringing and educational privileges, has not really come into contact with violence. Later we will see that the toughs in Gunn's poetry are disturbed individuals in search of an identity. For the moment it is revealing to hear what Gunn has to say about violence:

I think we live in an extremely unviolent world really. I know this is not the cliche, but if you compare somebody's day in London, say, or in San Francisco now with what it would have been 100 years ago let alone 200 years ago it's extraordinarily mild and easy and pacific—you don't see any fights around you or anything. I think our particular generation is obsessed with the idea of violence—maybe it misses it—it's a kind of nostalgia for violence. I think it's terribly unhealthy like most nostalgias. I think it's a nostalgia for something it hasn't ever had and doesn't particularly want really, wouldn't particularly like it if it had it, but it is around us. I suppose I'm rather typical in this way. I'm trying to be a bit more intelligent about it in [My Sad Captains] and what I'm writing now but I suppose I was extremely typical of the 50s in what I was writing.[6]

5 *London Magazine*, January 1971, pp. 5–7.
6 From the record, *The Poet Speaks*, London (Argo PLP 1085) 1965.

3

That is the voice of the middle-class man who can afford to live in unviolent areas. That is the voice of the man far enough from the thugly crowd to be in a different world from them. Gunn's assertion that contemporary society is 'mild and easy and pacific' will not bear examination. No fights in London? Some would disagree. As for San Francisco, where Gunn has chosen to make his home, here is a typical day:

> The afternoon newspaper reports the outbreak of a gang war in Chinatown, where an assassin is described as about 15 years old....A black man...broke into the home of a young white couple, battered the bound husband to death, raped his wife for three hours and then set fire to the house....A detective is suspended for shooting a 12-year-old black child....[7]

It is important to see Gunn and Hughes not as poets of violence but as poets whose struggle has been to break out of a stifling literary atmosphere. Gunn can indulge his sense of the histrionic by saying

> I think of all the toughs through history
> And thank heaven they lived, continually.
>> ('Lines for a Book', *The Sense of Movement*)

and have to apologise for it by telling a critic 'there is a kind of weakness in the attitude behind "Lines for a Book" because ultimately it can lead to Fascism, can't it?[8] Hughes can write a poem about a hawk saying

> There is no sophistry in my body:
> My manners are tearing off heads—
>> ('Hawk Roosting', *Lupercal*)

and feel obliged to complain to a critic 'That bird is accused of being a fascist...the symbol of some horrible totalitarian genocidal dictator'.[9] It is only in the context of the Eng. Lit. poetry seminar

7 Colin Smith, 'The City of Bad Dreams', *The Observer*, 12 May 1974, p. 29.
8 *London Magazine*, November 1964, p. 66.
9 *London Magazine*, January 1971, p. 8.

that such lines are capable of being considered violent, which is a criticism of English criticism, not of the poetry of Thom Gunn and Ted Hughes.

What Gunn and Hughes do have in common is the conviction that man's ability to act positively and with purpose is handicapped by his habit of perpetual reflection—of 'thinking too precisely on th'event', as Shakespeare put it in *Hamlet*. Both poets celebrate instinctive action and portray man burdened by his ability to perceive a multitude of choice. Unlike an animal, man cannot rely on a built-in purpose. Unlike an animal, man does not have a clear function: he has the appetites of the animal but the aspirations of a god. If man were like Gunn's werewolf 'Only to instinct and the moon being bound' ('The Allegory of the Wolf Boy', *The Sense of Movement*), or like Hughes's fox 'Coming about its own business' ('The Thought Fox', *The Hawk in the Rain*), there would not be all that much left for them to write about. This may be a limitation but it is one that is rooted in the limitations of man as a species. Out of this contradiction—man the almost animal, man the potential God—they have made a poetry of extremes and meta-morphoses. Man's aspiration to be a god leaves an imaginative blank which Gunn fills with human creations like the city, 'Extreme, material, and the work of man' ('In Praise of Cities', *The Sense of Movement*), while Hughes contrasts the functional lifeforce of animals with man's 'indolent procrastinations and... yawning stares' ('Thrushes', *Lupercal*).

It will be the contention of this book that, while the work of Gunn and Hughes makes an illuminating contrast, they do not have much in common either in motivation or achievement. They are two distinct poetic entities. Take the first poem in the authorised version of Thom Gunn's first book, *Fighting Terms* (1954)—that is the Faber edition of February 1962, not the Fantasy Press edition which Gunn revised—'The Wound' which opens with a seemingly violent image:

> The huge wound in my head began to heal
> About the beginning of the seventh week.
> Its valleys darkened, its villages became still:
> For joy I did not move and dared not speak;
> Nor doctors would cure it, but time, its patient skill.

Yet look at the image of the wound closely: it is immediately contained inside a familiar poetic idiom. The first line is pure iambic pentameter, the most recognisable rhythm in English poetry. And the whole statement emerges from a simple stanzaic pattern of *a b a b a*. So what is new is being delivered in an old bottle. Or, to change images, the picture might be modern and psychological but the frame that contains it is old and respectable and dignified through loving care.

The first poem in Ted Hughes's first book—the title poem from *The Hawk in the Rain* (1957)—is something much more disturbing and energetic. The language is impulsive and the poet seems more possessed by his material than in control of it. Whereas Gunn is laying out his images in an orderly, consecutive way, Hughes seems at the mercy of the powerful imagery inside him:

> I drown in the drumming ploughland, I drag up
> Heel after heel from the swallowing of the earth's mouth,
> From clay that clutches my each step to the ankle
> With the habit of the dogged grave....

Forget the influence of Hopkins and Dylan Thomas: this is a poetry devoid of charm, the poetry of a man possessed by his subject-matter.

Neither Thom Gunn nor Ted Hughes has sought publicity about his private life. Gunn, for example, says 'I am not "confessional" by nature, and I think too much biography is going to distort a poem rather than otherwise. It has always struck me as one of the many virtues of Shakespeare that he left us no life to speak of.'[10] Hughes is characteristically blunt on the subject of personal details: 'What can one say that isn't just blather, unless it's entertainment.'[11] Inevitably, however, public fame has led to a certain invasion of the poets' privacy.

Thom Gunn's life has been one of response to his times in many ways. His life has been a teleological one in the sense that it has moved from contented childhood to happy adulthood without much incident. He has been to school, done his National Service, studied at Cambridge, taught at Stanford, and dropped out of

10 Letter, 21 January 1973.
11 Letter, 10 November 1973.

teaching to 'do his own thing' (as they, in San Francisco, were the first to say): namely poetry. Ted Hughes has lived through an internationally publicised tragedy—the suicide of his first wife, Sylvia Plath, in 1963—and has had to bear with the endless literary post mortems ever since. The pages of this chapter seek to show what kind of people these two poets are without seeking to explain away the poetry in biographical details.

Thomson William Gunn was born 29 August 1929 in Gravesend, a market town in Kent on the Thames estuary. His mother, Ann Charlotte Thomson, the daughter of a tenant farmer, died when he was 14. His father, Herbert Smith Gunn, the son of a merchant seaman, died 2 March 1962 at the age of 57. Herbert Gunn was a very successful journalist and, like Thom, was born in Gravesend. He trained on the *Kent Messenger* and the year Thom was born he was sub-editor on the London *Evening News*. He became a sub-editor on the London *Evening Standard* in 1931, its news editor from 1933–6 then—after two years in Manchester and six years in London with the *Daily Express*—he was appointed editor of the *Evening Standard* in 1944. Of this appointment the historian A.J.P. Taylor has written:

> As the end of the war approached, Beaverbrook looked forward with pleasure to a renewal of party strife, and it became increasingly difficult for him to maintain the *Evening Standard* as a left wing paper. Michael Foot ceased to be its editor, being succeeded by a safe man, Herbert Gunn.[12]

Not all that safe, however, for Herbert Gunn fell out with Beaverbrook in 1950 when he tried to convince his employer that the *Evening Standard* should be made more sensational. In this context we might note that Gunn lists his recreation in *Who's Who* as 'cheap thrills'.

When Thom was eight his family settled in Hampstead. He played with friends on fashionable Hampstead Heath and enjoyed reading Beatrix Potter and E. Nesbit. He was a conventional middle class child. In view of his later celebration of tearaways I

12 A.J.P. Taylor, *Beaverbrook*, London (Hamish Hamilton) 1972, Penguin edition (1974) p. 705.

asked Gunn if he had been fascinated by the aggressive power of working class boys. He replied:

> I was quite a self-enclosed middle-class boy till the death of my mother when I was 14; after which I spent about half the year in Hampstead and the other half with aunts in Snodland, Kent, where I worked on their milk round quite often. So I never had any notions about class other than that it was something to be disregarded as much as possible.[13]

He was educated at University College school except for four terms at Bedales during the Blitz. It should be remembered that Gunn was ten when the war broke out so that his early teenage years were immersed in tales about the Second World War. Not only that, there were soldiers to be seen and Gunn liked what he saw. As a poet he has always used the image of the soldier for a man with a definite identity. The soldier does not agonisingly philosophise about his existential potentiality: he obeys orders. Gunn's leather-jacketed motor cyclists try to affect a military uniform. This fascination with soldiers began when Gunn was 'about fourteen or so/And my passion and concern was death' as he says in a poem called 'The Corporal' from his book *To the Air*:

> Half of my youth I watched the soldiers
> And saw mechanic clerk and cook
> Subsumed beneath a uniform.
> Grey black and khaki was their look
> Whose tool and instrument was death.

Side by side with this fascination with soldiers was a love-affair with literature. According to Herbert Smith Gunn, Thom was better read at the age of 11 than most people at 35.[14] So while half of him identified with the soldiers whose uniform dignified them with a definite identity, the other half was a bookish dreamer. In an uncollected poem 'Autobiography' he remembers

---

13 Letter, 21 January 1973.
14 *The Times Educational Supplement*, 3 August 1956, p. 995.

> how it felt
> to sit on Parliament
> Hill on a May evening
> studying for exams skinny
> seventeen. . . .

From this reverie Gunn was plucked in 1948 when his country needed him to do two years National Service. Basic training exhilarated him but the routine life of the National Serviceman bored him rigid for two years. There was little to do but read and Gunn passed his time with Marcel Proust's seven-volume psychological epic *A la recherche du temps perdu* (1913–26). After spending his time absorbing Proust's concept of time Gunn thought he might emulate his master. When he finished with the army he decided to write a Proustian novel. So he went to Paris to get on with it.

In Paris Gunn got a job in the office of the Metro. After work he got down to his Proustian novel. But he found he was losing himself in a mass of psychological insights and complicated syntax. He may even have become bored with Proust for in *My Sad Captains* an epigrammatic poem 'Readings in French' contains this observation:

> *Nothing Unusual about Marcel Proust*
> All are unmasked as perverts sooner or later,
> With a notable exception—the narrator.

He abandoned his novel, gave up fiction, took up poetry. He felt the discipline of the medium, its formal restraints, would enable him to express ideas and images with clarity and precision. Subsequent poetic achievements have justified his decision.

In 1950 Gunn went up to Trinity College, Cambridge, to read English and write poetry. He contributed poems to the undergraduate magazines, edited *Poetry from Cambridge 1951–1952* (1952) and in 1954, the year of his graduation, the Fantasy Press brought out his first book, *Fighting Terms*. Of Cambridge he has said: 'As for Cambridge: yes, I grew up there—rapidly, in the years 21 to 23. It was very important to me, I was influenced by everybody and everything I came in contact with.'[15] One of the people he didn't come into contact with was Ted Hughes:

> At Cambridge we barely knew each other. I'm not sure we even met when we were there, though I certainly knew him by sight. And since then we've never been long enough in the same place to know each other really well. I admire his poetry enormously and I find him a man of tremendous warmth.[16]

After graduating Gunn spent some months in Rome on a studentship then got a poetry fellowship at Stanford University. In his first year at Stanford he worked under the poet and critic Yvor Winters (1900–1968) whose influence led Gunn to a more thorough consideration of the concept of will. In a poem 'To Yvor Winters, 1955' Gunn has said:

> You keep both Rule and Energy in view,
> Much power in each, most in the balanced two:
> Ferocity existing in the fence
> Built by an exercised intelligence.

After a year in Texas Gunn returned to Stanford to read for a Ph.D. but the work bored him and he gladly accepted a teaching post at the University of California, Berkeley, in 1958. In 1960 he settled in San Francisco where he still lives.

In 1959 Gunn's *The Sense of Movement* appeared to wide acclamation. In 1961 *My Sad Captains* showed Gunn using syllabic verse and seeming more American, less English. In 1964 he returned to London to work with Ander, his photographer brother, on a book combining visual and verbal elements. By the time *Positives* (1966) appeared, Gunn had dropped out of teaching. Since then he has lived by lecturing occasionally and by giving poetry readings. In 1967 *Touch* appeared, containing Gunn's most ambitious poem 'Misanthropos'. For Gunn 1971 was the year of *Moly*. Thus six books—*Fighting Terms* (1954), *The Sense of Movement* (1957), *My Sad Captains* (1961), *Positives* (1966), *Touch* (1967), *Moly* (1971)—are the basis on which his reputation rests at the present.

15 Letter, 17 March 1974.
16 *Ibid.*

To date Ted Hughes has published even fewer books aimed at the general public—that is large, not limited, editions. His reputation rests on four books: *The Hawk in the Rain* (1957), *Lupercal* (1960), *Wodwo* (1967) and *Crow* (1970). Despite this relatively small output few poets have such an international reputation as Ted Hughes.

Edward J. Hughes, a carpenter's son, was born 17 August 1930 in Mytholmroyd, a little town in the West Riding of Yorkshire. Ted was the third of three children. His father, William Hughes, became a sergeant in World War One where he witnessed the disastrous result of the allied landing on the Gallipoli peninsula in April 1915. It made a lasting impression on him and he filled Ted's childhood with tales of the horrors of the war.

His emphasis on World War One had a permanent effect on Hughes who has written many pieces explicitly about a World War which was history twelve years before he was born. In *The Hawk in the Rain* there are poems like 'The Casualty', 'Bayonet Charge', 'Griefs for Dead Soldiers', 'Six Young Men', 'Two Wise Generals'; there is the sequence 'Scapegoats and Rabies' (published in a limited edition in 1965 but included in the American edition of *Wodwo* and in *Selected Poems 1957–67*); in *Wodwo* there is the poem 'Bowled Over' and the radio play 'The Wound'. In his childhood Hughes must have imaginatively experienced World War One in a particularly intense way.

The second enduring influence on Ted Hughes has been the influence of the West Riding landscape. Mytholmroyd, Hughes's birthplace in the Calder Valley, is seven miles from Haworth as the crow flies. And Haworth is where the Brontës lived.

The Pennines are seductively sensuous hills from a distance but to be on them is to be at the mercy of the weather. And Pennine weather has a filthy temper. It is capable of blasting cold wind at individuals who stand up to it, more than likely to inflict driving rain. Hughes's poetry is permeated with memories of rain: 'And rain hacks my head to the bone.' ('The Hawk in the Rain', *Wodwo*): 'Winds stampeding the fields under the window/Floundering black astride and blinding wet' ('Wind', *The Hawk in the Rain*); 'Rain plastered the land till it was shining/Like hammered lead' ('November', *Lupercal*); 'Only the rain never tires' ('Heptonstall', *Woodwo*); 'Slowly a hundred miles through the powerful rain'

('You Drive in a Circle', *Wodwo*). His respect for the power of nature is a hallmark of his poetry. In this he is a true product of the West Riding.

From the beginning Hughes was fascinated by animals:

> My interest in animals began when I began. My
> memory goes back pretty clearly to my third year, and
> by then I had so many of the toy lead animals you
> could buy in shops that they went right round our flat-
> topped fender, nose to tail, with some over.[17]

Nor was he content with toy animals, but intent on capturing real ones: live mice at threshing time, dead owls and magpies and rabbits shot by his elder brother Gerald when the two roamed the hillsides together. It was a challenging environment, one that put man in his place, a constant reminder of the struggle for survival in the animal kingdom. Yet the West Riding not only gave Hughes a respect for the elements and an opportunity to live among animals. There was also the dialect:

> They have a very distinctive dialect there.... Without
> it, I doubt if I would ever have written verse. And in
> the case of the West Yorkshire dialect, of course, it
> connects you directly and in your most intimate self to
> middle English poetry.[18]

When Hughes was seven the family moved to Mexborough, a coalmining town in south Yorkshire. It was an upheaval, a move from rural to urban life. Hughes's parents took a newsagent's and tobacconist's shop and settled down. Ted's brother Gerald could not, however, tolerate the ways of a small industrial town: he left home to become a gamekeeper. Hughes himself made friends with the town boys but, more importantly, found somewhere he could indulge his appetite for solitude, his empathy with animals. There was a farm in the country near Mexborough where Hughes could rediscover his relationship with natural things. There was also a private estate with woods to wander in and lakes to linger over.

17 Hughes, *Poetry in the Making*, London (Faber & Faber) 1967, p. 15.
18 *London Magazine*, January 1971, p. 11–2.

Hughes came to feel that 'in many ways that move of ours was the best thing that ever happened to me'.[19]

Hughes attended Mexborough Grammar School and, in 1948, won an Open Exhibition in English to Pembroke College, Cambridge. Before going up to university he did two years National Service as an RAF ground wireless mechanic in east Yorkshire. Like National Serviceman Thom Gunn, National Serviceman Ted Hughes found he had very little to do but pass the time. This he did by concentrating on Shakespeare. He had read so much that by the time he got to Cambridge he could not fully enter into the spirit of the English course. He did two years of it then, in his third year, switched to Archaeology and Anthropology. A Cambridge contemporary, Wendy Campbell, remembers Ted Hughes the student:

> He lived with such vehemence, and such a perfect absence of self-consciousness, and such a total indifference to the modes of the Establishment that it was not always easy to preserve both Ted and the appearances which were thought to be necessary. . . Ted was not only physically large, but he had a corresponding largeness of being. He was unfettered; he was unafraid; he didn't care, in a tidy bourgeois sense, he didn't care a damn for anyone or anything.[20]

Be that as it may, Hughes graduated in 1954, but not to go into academic life.

> After a spell of tramping here and there, and another driving an uncle round the continent, I took a job as a rose-gardener, then as a night-watchman in a steel factory in London, and later as a reader for J. Arthur Rank at the Pinewood Studios.
>
> In the winter of 1955 I met Sylvia Plath, a 1955 graduate from Smith College, on a Fulbright grant at Newnham College, Cambridge. She had published

19 Hughes, *Poetry in the Making*, London (Faber & Faber) 1967, p. 16.
20 *The Art of Sylvia Plath*, ed. Charles Newman, London (Faber & Faber) 1970, pp. 183–4.

poems and stories. . .and began to send my poems
around. We were married [on 16 June 1956]. After a
summer spent writing in Spain, we came back to
Cambridge, where I began teaching in a secondary
modern school while Sylvia finished her English
Tripos. . . . We are spending this summer writing on
Cape Cod, after which we will proceed to Northampton,
Massachusetts, where Sylvia has a job as instructor of
freshman English at Smith College. We both plan to
combine writing and teaching in America.[21]

Hughes wrote that note in 1957. He was confident that he and
Sylvia Plath could launch a powerful husband-and-wife literary
team, and indeed 1957 was a good year for them. Sylvia turned
out to be an excellent teacher and Ted's first book, *The Hawk in the
Rain*, won him prizes and enormous critical acclaim. In 1959 he
was awarded a Guggenheim Fellowship and used it to travel across
the USA with his wife.

The Hugheses returned to England in 1959, found a little flat in
London, and had their first child, Frieda Rebecca, in 1960. That
was also a good year. Hughes's second book, *Lupercal*, confirmed
his stature as a young poet of enormous promise. The same year
Sylvia Plath's *The Colossus* was published. With hindsight we know
that her legend was beginning.

When, in 1961, the Hugheses moved to an old manor house in
North Tawton, Devon, they had a brilliant future ahead of them.
A second child, Nicholas Ferrer, was born there in 1962. Soon
afterwards, however, the couple separated. Sylvia and the two
children moved to a flat near Primrose Hill in London. On 11
February 1963 Sylvia Plath gassed herself in this flat. Ted Hughes's
suspicion of the destructive forces at large in the world had been
tragically confirmed. What impact Sylvia Plath's suicide had on
Ted Hughes is something he is not prepared to discuss. It is
therefore a matter for idle speculation. What should be mentioned
is that Hughes published no major book for four years after his
wife's suicide. Instead he concentrated on children's books: *The
Earth Owl and Other Moon People* (1963), *How the Whale Became*

21 Note written by Hughes for the Halifax *Evening Courier*, filed 10 December
1957.

(1963), *Nessie the Mannerless Monster* (1964). When *Wodwo* came out in 1967 it showed Hughes increasingly moving into realms of nightmare imagery.

In 1970 Hughes married Carole Orchard and published *Crow*. This book is probably the most discussed collection of English poetry to appear since the days of Dylan Thomas. Some have found it repulsive, some a work of genius. It is certainly impossible to ignore now that it is there.

But before coming to the later work of Hughes and Gunn it is necessary to see what led up to it and whether there has been progression or regression. The next chapter examines the wilful Gunn of *Fighting Terms*, *The Sense of Movement* and *My Sad Captains*. In the third chapter the naturalistic animal-orientated Hughes of *The Hawk in the Rain* and *Lupercal* makes his presence felt. Gunn's more humane aspects—as displayed in *Positives*, *Touch* and *Moly*—are discussed in the fourth chapter. This accent to sunnier moods is diametrically opposed by the nightmarish world of Hughes's *Wodwo* and *Crow* which dominates the fifth chapter.

2 'All the Toughs'

When the general public thinks of poets it generally thinks of dreamers, men who have time to stand and stare while the rest of the world works, introverts who recollect small emotions in languorous tranquillity.

Thom Gunn wanted to reverse the connotations that stuck to the poet like embarrassing bits of confetti. He wanted to impose a pattern on nature, to secure a firm, demonstrative identity for himself, to demonstrate a trained mind, not a sloppy one. In pursuit of this goal he kicked about with motorcyclists while retaining a tight, disciplined control of his poetry.

That this was a deliberate literary decision on the part of Gunn can best be seen by the way in which his revolt into a wilful style is staged in entirely literary terms. Gunn, the poet of choice, chose a poetic role for himself just as surely as motorcyclists in the 1950s chose the pseudo-military trappings of leather jackets, boots and goggles. Stephen Spender, an archetypal upper class sensitive plant of a poet, has an autobiographical poem called 'Rough' which tells how

> My parents kept me from children who were rough
> Who threw words like stones and who wore torn clothes.
> Their thighs showed through rags. They ran in the
>   street
> And climbed cliffs and stripped by the country streams.

(Incidentally such confessions of childhood timidity are quite common in modern English poetry: Donald Davie, for example, has a poem on 'Barnsley and District' which tells how 'I ran and ran from colliers' boys in jerseys, Wearing a blouse to show my finer feelings.') Spender tells how he 'feared more than tigers their muscles like iron.' On the face of it Gunn has much in common with

Spender. Gunn lived in Hampstead, one of the poshest parts of London. He went to University College school. And he has said that he was 'quite a self-enclosed middle class boy till the death of my mother when I was 14.'[1] Yet Gunn is determined to dissociate himself from the likes of Spender. So he wrote a poem called 'Lines for a Book' which caused considerable controversy when it appeared in *The Sense of Movement*:

> I think of all the toughs through history
> And thank heaven they lived, continually.
> I praise the overdogs from Alexander
> To those who would not play with Stephen Spender.

The point about such lines is that they would be completely lost on a tough (who might have vaguely heard of Alexander, but hardly of Stephen Spender) but easily grasped by an aesthete. So Gunn's poems in praise of toughness are intended for poetry-reading non-toughs. Gunn's hobby is weight-lifting but he has never completely succeeded in throwing off the weight of the university-made literary tradition that hangs over his head.

It is a bit premature to speak of an early and late manner in so young a poet as Gunn (at the time of writing he is 45). Still, his first three collections of poetry—*Fighting Terms*, *The Sense of Movement* and the first part of *My Sad Captains*—do constitute a definite phase in his work. This period is concerned with eulogising the man of action, emphasising the necessity of will and discipline, searching for a definite personal identity (a motorcyclist's badge of courage). This is no arbitrary division, as we have it on Gunn's own authority that the title poem of *My Sad Captains*, the closing poem in the book, 'rounds off this part of my poetry, poetry in much of which I emphasise the will as an end in itself.'[2] These three books glorify the man of action at the expense of the thinker, describe human relationships in images drawn from military strategy, and generally stress the masculine qualities of hardness, brute insensitivity and physical presence. In 'Lines for a Book'—a credo for the early Gunn—we have a plan of mental action:

1 Letter, 21 January 1973.
2 Letter, 7 October 1972.

> It's better
> To go and see your friend than write a letter;
> To be a soldier than to be a cripple;
> To take an early weaning from the nipple
> Than think your mother is the only girl;
> To be insensitive, to steel the will,
> Than sit irresolute all day at stool
> Inside the heart.

Gunn's first book, *Fighting Terms*, was published by the Fantasy Press in 1954 when the poet was 25. It was revised for an edition published by New York's Hawk's Well Press in 1959, then re-revised and restored for the Faber edition of February 1962. It is this edition, the one authorised by Gunn, that we shall consider. Technically, the poetry in *Fighting Terms* is conventional, using regular stanzaic and rhyming patterns and relying for rhythm almost exclusively on the iambic pentameter, the rhythm that served Shakespeare and Donne. What is uniquely Gunnish in the book is the dependence on an imagery of assault. Gunn presents combatants, not passive observers, and justifies the belligerent title of the book by his military allusions: 'I fought in turn' ('The Wound'); 'the mesh/Of the continual battle's sound' ('Helen's Rape'); 'shot the muffled stranger in the head' ('The Right Possessor'); 'Fighting before and after, through your land' ('The Beach Head'); 'His forehead had a bloody wound' ('Incident on a Journey'). At its most successful this has the effect of giving the narrative poems a dynamic quality, at worst it is like an overgrown boy playing with toy soldiers.

The first poem in *Fighting Terms*, 'The Wound', is also the best. Gunn certainly thinks 'this is the best poem in my first book...I think I was hiding irritation beneath the heroic, or maybe trying to translate it into the heroic'.[3] Ostensibly the poem is spoken by a wounded soldier who has fought on both sides of the Trojan war and been wounded:

> The huge wound in my head began to heal
> About the beginning of the seventh week.

3 *Ibid.*

From this arresting opening Gunn introduces a dynamic of positive action: 'I fought', 'sallied out/Each day with Hector', 'the lout/Thersites', 'I called for armour', 'rage at his noble pain'. However this remains the poem of a man who has read—and responded imaginatively—to Shakespeare's *Troilus and Cressida*, not the poem of a man who has suffered physical pain. On closer inspection the poem is not about physical violence at all, but about mental anguish. The headwound is a metaphor for mental agony. With his decision to avoid blatant confession of despair Gunn is to be congratulated on finding such an effective objective correlative for the despair of a young man. He has transformed the torment of the sensitive man (and Gunn is a sensitive man) into a metaphorical wound inflicted by others. Throughout Gunn's work there is this feeling that man is incapacitated, wounded by his consciousness of moral choices, by his sense of belonging to a species which insists on normative behaviour.

Technically, 'The Wound' is a formal piece of writing. Written in five five-line stanzas rhyming *a b a b a* it shows Gunn already settling in to his beloved iambic pentameter: 'For joy I did not move and dared not speak', 'I lay and rested as prescription said', 'I called for armour, rose, and did not reel'. Some critics, keen to spot a contemporary influence on Gunn, called him Empsonian. Gunn however has denied this. 'My early poems looked like Empson', he has said, 'quite simply because I was influenced by some of the things he had been influenced by: the Cambridge English School, Donne, Auden.'[4] The temperamental reason for Gunn's use of Metaphysical matter in a traditional manner is surely that he wished to be completely in control of the poems he was creating. It would be ludicrous to pose as the poet of discipline and control in verse that fell apart at the edges. Yet the traditional style of Gunn's early poetry does give it a predictable texture. The reader knows that if a poem begins in iambic pentameter it is likely to go on like that all the way through. So there are no rhythmic surprises, simply the working out of a thought.

Just as *Fighting Terms* opens with a wounded man, so it closes with a similar character in 'Incident on a Journey': these two poems provide a blood-red frame for the poems that stretch

4 *The Times Educational Supplement*, 3 August 1956, p. 995.

between them. 'Incident on a Journey' opens in a cave where the poet does not act but sleeps until awoken by a man of action:

> One night I reached a cave: I slept, my head
> Full of the air. There came about daybreak
> A red-coat soldier to the mouth. who said
> 'I am not living, in hell's pains I ache,
> > *But I regret nothing.*'

A cave for Gunn is a metaphor for the stifling prison of inaction, of purely passive reflection. In an earlier poem in the book, 'Merlin in the Cave: He Speculates Without a Book', Merlin's bookishness has led him into 'the terrible cave . . . . The absolute prison'.

The reason for the soldier's agony is that 'His forehead had a bloody wound'. The soldier is Gunn's dream of himself as potentially a man of action but incapacitated by the intellectual headwound of anguish ('Whether his words were mine or his, in dreaming/I found they were my deepest thoughts translated'). Before receiving his headwound of anguish the soldier was an impulsive man of action of the type worshipped by Gunn:

> And always when a living impulse came
> I acted, and my action made me wise.
> > *And I regretted nothing.*

This heroic quality was lost when the soldier was wounded—forced to reflect—and became 'will-less' and 'feeble-limbed'. Incapable as he now is of acting on impulse, his wound has 'scattered instinct to the wind'. At this point the dreamer in Gunn awakes. He sees the way out of the cave his dreams have trapped him in. He will act, will his·body to achievement, throw off conventional morality:

> I was alive and felt my body sweet,
> Uncaked blood in all its channels flowing.
> > *I would regret nothing.*

The question that 'Incident on a Journey' leaves unanswered is just what constitutes meaningful action. It is not enough to say 'I acted, and my action made me wise' because an act could be an act of murder or an act of wanton destruction. Yet Gunn seems reluctant to define the nature of an action. What he is determined to state is that he will not 'sit irresolute all day at stool/Inside the heart', a negative resolution.

It is as if Gunn feels that, unless he makes an effort of will to escape from the dead hand of tradition, he might end up like a modern-day Lazarus, all lethargy and inertia. 'Lazarus Not Raised' reverses the biblical story. Gunn's Lazarus is not a physical corpse, but an intellectual zombie with a 'greasy placid face' incapable of breaking away from the secure confines of his childhood. Lazarus is incapable of real effort: 'He had chosen to stay dead'.

Gunn, with his immersion in words, cannot have failed to notice the twin connotations of acting: activity and pretence. So he begins 'Carnal Knowledge' by announcing 'Even In bed I pose'. Gunn's is very much a pre-Women's Liberation view of sex. Man takes the dominant role in a mechanical, ultimately meaningless activity:

> I prod you, you react. Thus to and fro
> We turn, to see ourselves perform the same
> Comical act inside the tragic game.

and again:

> Lie back. Within a minute I will stow
> Your greedy mouth, but will not yet to grips.
> 'There is a space between the breast and lips.'
> Also a space between the thighs and head,
> So great, we might as well not be in bed:
> For we learn nothing here we did not know.

Gunn's view of sex when it is not amusing is patently absurd. Sex is the action that sustains the species, an intense reciprocal activity, an interpenetration of personality. Only the most bookish man would go to bed to 'learn' something. Granted this is to read between the lines so literally as to be unfair, as the poem is meant to be an unfond farewell to a boring lover ('Your intellectual protests are a bore...so now go'). However, the arrogantly masculine attitude to sex is not confined to this poem.

The hero of 'Lofty in the Palais de Danse' is an ex-serviceman who spends each evening trying to find an equivalent for a girl he once loved and who has died. Like Gunn, Lofty is a seeker after truth, a modern Odysseus in search of the perfect Penelope. Like Gunn, he cannot find a girl who amounts to more than her body. Each girl is 'understood/Exhaustively as soon as slept with'. Women are seen as too soft, too inactive, too submissive, too cynically repetitive. Small wonder that Gunn could not follow Andrew Marvell in pleading 'To His Coy Mistress'. Gunn instead writes 'To His Cynical Mistress' and uses the image of love as a battlefield on which men and women indulge in hostilities. Love is 'An impermanent treaty waiting to be signed/By the two enemies'. Lovers are leaders of enemy factions in which 'The leaders calmly plot assassination'. It is an existential axiom that a sexual encounter with another's body confirms one's own existence but this does nothing to get Gunn out of the egocentric world in which, by the admission of several poems, he feels trapped.

The best of the antilove poems in *Fighting Terms* is 'The Beach Head'. This is a genuinely successful modern Metaphysical poem in the sense that Gunn is extremely adroit at sustaining the military metaphor throughout the poem to the extent that the imagery assumes an independent life of its own. A beach head is an area held on an enemy's shore for the purpose of penetrating into alien territory. Thus it is a perfect image of sexual exploration for Gunn. The poem is a verse epistle to a girl Gunn wants to possess and conquer completely so that her body becomes merely the first step to complete victory over her being. Her body is the enemy area on which he will make his assault. Because in this poem Gunn acknowledges more than physical desire he admits to having the headwound of anguish: he is a 'brain-sick enemy', a 'hare-brained stranger' seeking through the sexual act 'a pathway to the human heart'. To achieve this goal he threatens to come 'in one spectacular dash,/Fighting before and after, through your land' and only holds back because 'Hurry is blind and so does not brave mystery'. By taking his time Gunn will be unlike other rivals for the girl's being, he will be individual. The language of 'The Beach Head' is vigorous and this is the best example of Gunn's revitalisation of the iambic pentameter in *Fighting Terms*, plenty of enjambement, many unpredictable rhymes:

Now that a letter gives me ground at last
For starting from, I see my enterprise
Is more than application by a blast
Upon a trumpet slung beside a gate,
Security a fraud, and how unwise
Was disembarking on your Welfare State.

And yet the poem only promises action. Nothing physical actually
happens. The energy is confined to the Metaphysical conceits.
Nor has Gunn rid himself of his egocentricity for his fear is that he
'Would not be much distinguished from the rest'. His terror is of
being one of many, his ambition to be one among many. Which is
why the poem ends indecisively by opting for stealth and caution:
'And risk that your mild liking turn to loathing'.

To be fair to Gunn, he is on record as saying that *Fighting Terms*
'bears all the marks of the undergraduate writer, and if there is
anything to be claimed for it it must be the spontaneity of its awk-
wardness'.[5] It is a strange mixture of emotional immaturity and
technical assurance.

'Tamer and Hawk' describes the poet under the control of a
dominant mistress, yet it does so with a fine melancholy cadence
and an energy lurking underneath the resignation:

I thought I was so tough,
But gentled at your hands
Cannot be quick enough
To fly for you and show
That when I go I go
At your commands.

This is followed by two stanzas in which the idea of captivity is
developed so the hawk is 'no longer free', 'blind to other birds'
because

The habit of your words
Has hooded me.

5 Autobiographical note written for Faber & Faber, November 1972.

which is a striking pun on 'habit' as both behavioural repetition and engulfing garment. On top of that the poem ends with a mild shock-effect. Because the hawk is kept under close watch it must finally turn on the only bait around: the tamer. This would make a neat comment on many a human relationship.

Fighting Terms thus shows Gunn to be a man at odds with himself. He is capable of moralising about nations while at the same time expressing contempt for those willing to love him. He exalts action above reflection yet is himself a most reflective poet, an activist only of the intellect. Gunn is conscious of this and in 'For a Birthday' (he was 25 when the book was published, a quarter of a century old) claims that 'I have reached a time when words no longer help'. What he dislikes about words is the way they classify emotion, the way they automatically relate an experience to a precedent. The intellectual catalogues each emotion, relates particulars to a general concept of behaviour, so that it becomes almost impossible to embrace fresh sensations. What Gunn wants is a way to break through the barriers that words and concepts impose on the individual. He would like to recreate imaginatively a world uncontaminated by classification. After all he has said about sex he seems ready to admit that the road to this freshness lies along the sacramental road of love:

> All my agnostic irony I renounce
> So I may climb to regions where I rest
> In springs of speech, the dark before of truth:
> The sweet moist wafer of your tongue I taste,
> And find right meanings in your silent mouth.

After leaving Cambridge Gunn spent a few months in Rome on a studentship and then went to Stanford University to take up a fellowship. So he did not, after all, take the way of the man of action but went back to the academically-orientated life.

> I worked under Yvor Winters my first year at Stanford, and my second book is equally influenced by his poetry and by Jean-Paul Sartre's plays. I made much use of the word 'will' in this book. It is a favourite word also of Winters and of Sartre, but they each meant something

very different, and would have understood but not
admitted the other's use of it. I suspect that what I
meant by it was a mere Yeatsian wilfulness.[6]

This demonstrated that Gunn was still drawing the deepest
sources of his inspiration from books and from academics.

Be that as it may, his second book, *The Sense of Movement*,
published in June 1957, contains much that is impressive. It has
an obsessive quality about it that gives it the hallmark of authen-
ticity. However unpleasant some of the details in the book, they
are part of Thom Gunn. *The Sense of Movement* is his portrait of his
personality as it was at the age of 27—warts and all. It is now
available in paperback but I have a feeling that a future definitive
edition will be tightly bound in leather, with a buckle for a clasp,
so that readers can appreciate in full its fetishistic character:
'gleaming jackets.... They strap in doubt' ('On the Move'):
'Other smells,/Horses, leather, manure, fresh sweat' ('At the Back
of the North Wind'); 'Strapped helpless' ('The Wheel of Fortune'):
'He grips your arm like a cold strap of leather' ('The Silver Age'):
'he buckles himself in, with bootstraps and Marine belt' ('Market
at Turk'); 'the tools of their perversity,/Whip, cords, and strap'
('The Beaters'): 'no use for his whip, I work so hard' ('Legal
Reform').

The Sense of Movement contains 32 poems and, besides the touches
of leather fetishism, there is the obsessional interest in the will.
This catalogue is almost as revealing as the last one: 'the created
will' ('On the Move'); 'My cause lay in the will' ('The Nature of
an Action'); 'My human will' ('The Unsettled Motorcyclist's
Vision of his Death'); 'To steel the will' ('Lines for a Book'):
'reminders of the will' ('Market at Turk'); 'hoarded against his
will' ('The Allegory of the Wolf Boy'); 'the pure will' ('Julian the
Apostate'); 'the deliberate human will' ('To Yvor Winters'). In
The Sense of Movement the will is the machine that drives the body
into action. The body itself is an instrument that seeks an identity.

'On the Move', the first poem in the book, is already a classic of
the 1950s. It is the one poem of Gunn that every reader of modern
poetry knows. It is also the poem where he metaphorically trans-

6 *Ibid.*

forms his beloved motorcycle into a haunting image of the will to
self-expression. Gunn himself thinks that 'On the Move' is 'the
poem where I most expanded my range.'[7] It is a philosophical
poem, a meditation on a 'part solution' to the aimlessness of much
of modern life. Deliberately, Gunn has kept the narrative bones of
the poem to an absolute minimum so that if the will exists it will
be seen in this poem.

The poet is in north California and he watches a gang of
motorcyclists roar along the highway scaring 'a flight of birds
across the field'. Birds, however, act on animal instinct whereas
man's latent instinct has been vitiated by his intellect, his capacity
for doubt, by 'thinking too precisely on th'event', by habitually
questioning each impulse. So the motorcycle gang of the poem, the
Boys, are not to be thought of as mindless tearaways. As members
of the human species—albeit uneducated and sensation-seeking—
they are still to be credited with vastly more intellect than 'a flight
of birds'. One critic found it 'hard to share [Gunn's] uncritical
sympathy for nihilistic young tearaways in black leather jackets';[8]
yet that same critic would no doubt happily consider a poem about
the habits of 'a flight of birds' (as long as it was not a poem like
Ted Hughes's 'Thrushes'). The Boys are representatives of
humanity, however flawed, and their collective action has therefore
great interest and significance. They have found 'a part solution,
after all'. They have chosen to lose their individuality by conform-
ing to a code. They have chosen to become uniformed units, not
tormented individuals.

Gunn has admitted to me that the philosophical ideas behind
'On the Move' were 'lifted from Sartre's lecture *L'Existentialisme
est un humanisme*'.[9] In this lecture Sartre argued that the individual
can only be genuinely free by guaranteeing the freedom of others.
The pursuit of individual freedom without regard to other people
results in escapism:

> When a man commits himself to anything, fully realising
> that he is not only choosing what he will be, but is

7 Letter, 7 October 1972.
8 Kenneth Allott, *The Penguin Book of Contemporary Verse*, Harmondsworth
(Penguin Books) 2nd edn. 1962, p. 373.
9 Letter, 7 October 1972.

thereby at the same time a legislator deciding for the whole of mankind—in such a moment a man cannot escape from the sense of complete and profound responsibility. There are many, indeed, who show no such anxiety. But we affirm that they are merely disguising their anguish or are in flight from it.[10]

In this existentialist sense the Boys are disguising their anguish at their individual inadequacy by donning an aggressive uniform and are certainly 'in flight' from their anxiety:

On motorcycles, up the road, they come:
Small, black, as flies hanging in heat, the Boys,
Until the distance throws them forth, their hum
Bulges to thunder held by calf and thigh.
In goggles, donned impersonality,
In gleaming jackets trophied with the dust,
They strap in doubt—by hiding it, robust—
And almost hear a meaning in their noise.

Again Gunn is emphasising the human-ness of the Boys. They look like 'flies hanging in heat', they 'scare a flight of birds across the field' but it is as human beings that they feel the need to 'strap in doubt'. Flies and birds do not have doubts, humans do. Gunn has said

It is this malaise that I am trying to explore in most of the poems in *The Sense of Movement*...it seems to me a specifically contemporary subject; seeking to understand one's deliberate aimlessness, having the courage of one's lack of convictions, reaching a purpose only by making the right rejections. Poems are actions, of a sort, and by actions I may attempt to define the direction which is not mystical, or political, or necessarily one that has ever been taken before.[11]

10 Jean-Paul Sartre, *Existentialism and Humanism*, tr. Philip Mairet, London (Methuen) 1948, p. 30.
11 *Poetry Book Society Bulletin No 14*, London, May 1957.

The Boys are therefore engaged in demonstratively negative action, action that solves their egocentric dilemma. They have 'the courage of their lack of convictions'. Gunn has progressed technically from *Fighting Terms* but he is still advocating action for its own sake. The poem does not move beyond a statement of the powerful appearance of the Boys and an admittedly skilful communication of their anguish. Gunn credits them in eloquently ringing lines, with a 'part solution':

> It is a part solution, after all.
> One is not necessarily discord
> On earth; or damned because, half animal,
> One lacks direct instinct, because one wakes
> Afloat on movement that divides and breaks.
> One joins the movement in a valueless world,
> Choosing it, till, both hurler and the hurled,
> One moves as well, always toward, toward.

And yet these manifestations of existential anguish might well, in the nature of things, roar into a town and brutally rape some girls to the accompaniment of pathological giggling—or kick someone's face in. This 'part solution' is totally self-indulgent. It does not acknowledge the inviolability of other individuals.

The poem is beautifully composed in five eight-line stanzas rhyming *a b a c c d d b*. The fluency of the verse owes something to Wallace Stevens; while to Yeats Gunn owes details like 'bird nor holiness,/For birds and saints complete their purposes' and the cadence of the poem's conclusion:

> At worst, one is in motion; and at best,
> Reaching no absolute, in which to rest,
> One is always nearer by not keeping still

which echoes Yeats's 'The Second Coming':

> The ceremony of innocence is drowned;
> The best lack all conviction, while the worst
> Are full of passionate intensity.

Yeats is invoked again in another poem about motorcyclists, 'The Unsettled Motorcyclist's Vision of his Death', a title that recalls Yeat's 'An Irish Airman Foresees His Death' where the hero remembers how

> A lonely impulse of delight
> Drove to this tumult in the clouds.

Gunn's motorcyclist has a similar escapist motivation:

> Across the open countryside,
> Into the walls of rain I ride.
> It beats my cheek, drenches my knees,
> But I am being what I please.

Unlike the fluent 'On the Move', this poem is woodenly repetitive in rhythm. Of course, Gunn himself is the speaker in 'On the Move' while the motorcyclist narrator is a suicidally inclined sentimentalist. Nevertheless, twenty couplets of iambic tetrameter have more of the rhythm of the square-wheeled cart than the motorbike.

And when we get down to it 'being what I please' means, for the motorcyclist, a duel with nature:

> The firm heath stops, and marsh begins.
> Now we're at war: whichever wins
> My human will cannot submit
> To nature, though brought out of it.

He seems to get some pleasure out of the fact that, though the war with nature will end in his defeat, nature is 'mere embodiment'. Of the plants that will enter his corpse he observes that they have no human will:

> It is as servants they insist,
> Without volition that they twist;
> And habit does not leave them tired,
> By men laboriously acquired.

The intellectual content of this poem is frankly arrant nonsense. It glorifies the mentality of a crank. In everyday terms—and this is a test that can legitimately be applied to those poems by Gunn that claim to inhabit 'a specifically contemporary subject'—the motor-cyclist would be no tragic philosopher but simply a menace on the roads.

I have remarked already on Gunn's apparent inability to apprehend the true nature of violence, his fascination with the outward trappings only of violent men. 'Market at Turk' (Market and Turk are streets in San Francisco) operates on just such a superficial level. Its hero is a street corner thug. He has a knife which will presumably be used (once Gunn has done with the subject) on the human flesh of another human being. Yet Gunn sees this thug, too, as an unconscious exponent of existentialist philosophy. He is, though he does not know it, responding to the human need for action in his thuggishness while his outfit is an instant existential identity. Gunn is on safer ground with the purely simulated violence of the pop idol, in 'Elvis Presley'. Presley, in Gunn's poem, has the charismatic ability to invest the boring lot of modern youth with a fierce glamour:

> We keep ourselves in touch with a mere dime:
> Distorting hackneyed words in hackneyed songs
> He turns revolt into a style, prolongs
> The impulse to a habit of the time.

Elvis Presley is not the only hero in *The Sense of Movement*. There are, in fact, quite a galaxy of assorted characters: the werewolf, some sado-masochists, Emperor Julian the Apostate, the Virgin Mary, St. Martin, Yvor Winters, Puss in Boots, Merlin. They are all transformed into pillars supporting Gunn's pantheon. They are either capable of action or examples of inactivity. The werewolf of 'The Allegory of the Wolf Boy' is at first sight the familiar figure from the horror movies of the 1950s—the young lad who is reluctantly impelled into a horrific metamorphosis. The imagery, though second-hand, is handled expertly. This boy, like the Boys 'On the Move' is 'half animal'—only more so. He doesn't need an external uniform. He has his lunar identity, 'he hides in tissue/Seeds of division'. Like an animal he is 'Only to instinct and the moon being bound'. In short, every month he becomes an animal, a wolf. This does not solve anything, however, for he ends with 'bleeding paws': the animal half of him lacerates his human self. I think the clue to the 'bleeding paws' image is in the sleepy English rural gentility the werewolf moves in. He is present 'At tennis and at tea/Upon the gentle lawn'. It is this stifling conventional social background he breaks from when he

> Breaks from the house, wedges his clothes between
> Two moulded garden urns, and goes beyond
> His understanding.

He has 'bleeding paws' because he attacks his other self in anguish at the impossibility of ever escaping from the confines of his background. His is not even a 'part solution'. It is self destruction. The allegory is a sustained image of civilised English life acting like a vicious trap to squeeze all impulse and instinct out of the individual.

'The Beaters' is a nasty piece of work thinly disguised as a philosophically illustrative fable. The sadists in the poem have chosen 'limitation'. They are totally wrapped up in their own pursuit of pleasure yet able to give pleasure to a masochist who 'Can feel the pain sweet, tranquil, in his blood'. Gunn insists that such people are not mere perverts but are also individuals in search of an identity, philosophers in spite of themselves. But then for Gunn all men are philosophers to some degree, that being the unique characteristic of the human species. So sado-masochistic perversions become dignified by Gunn who sees them as examples of action:

> Ambiguous liberty! it is the air
> Between the raised arm and the fallen thud.

Here Gunn seems to me to have betrayed the aridity to which his intellectuality is prone. The concentration camps were full of people like 'The Beaters' and it is surely an abrogation of human concern to state that such people, too, can 'do their own thing' simply because it fits into his version of an existentialist view of things. Gunn does not necessarily admire the Beaters, but he rather naively gives them the benefit of the doubt.

Gunn can, in fact, be staggeringly naive and the surface sophistication of his poetry and vocabulary merely place an elaborate mask over the banality of poems like 'Market at Turk' or 'The Beaters'. They are academic poems in the worst sense of the term, mere exercises, versified anecdotes which hold a fascination for a poet who should know better. Gunn, in *The Sense of Movement*, is still searching for his own identity and the plethora of second-hand subjects he uses cannot disguise the fact. In 'Julian the Apostate' Gunn turns to the life of the fourth-century Roman emperor who renounced Christianity to revert to paganism. All Gunn contributes to this bit of potted history is the striking phrase 'the pure will of exclamation mark'. In 'Jesus and his Mother' Gunn simply alludes to the Gospel story—'twelve labouring men', 'speak with scholars in furred gown'—and has an uncomprehending Mary ask Jesus to behave like her son and not as the son of God. 'St. Martin and the Beggar' does not recreate or deeply explore the tale of the saint who divided his cloak with a beggar. Instead it retells the story in a parody of Auden's poem 'Victor. A Ballad':

> Martin sat young upon his bed
> A budding cenobite,
> Said, 'Though I hold the principles
> Of Christian life be right....

The finest love poem in *The Sense of Movement* is not addressed to a woman, however, but to the city, a beautiful realm of perpetual possibilities conceived in indifference. 'In Praise of Cities' indicates that Gunn finds the exploration of cities more rewarding than the exploration of other individuals because in them he can escape a definite commitment to another person. The city accepts him for what he is and asks nothing from him except his imposing presence. The city is 'Casual yet urgent in her love making,/She constantly asserts her independence'. She is like a prostitute who gives herself and leaves the lover with all his options open:

> She wanders lewdly, whispering her given name,
> Charing Cross Road, or Forty-Second Street:
> The longest streets, desire that never ends,

> Familiar and inexplicable, wearing
> Cosmetic light a fool could penetrate.

In other words Gunn is still keeping himself very much to himself and the poems still centre round his ego. The problem of perception, so attractive to post-Kantian philosophers, concerns the demarcation between the individual and the world around him. How much of it is independent from him, how much a projection of his perceptive faculties? Without the intervention of the ego objects can become contemptibly familiar, so in 'The Nature of an Action' Gunn tells how the world of objects means little for him until he can impose an order on them from the shape of his ego. He recalls his journey through 'the narrow corridor'— a metaphor for his sheltered, bookish life—when he

> Doubted myself, what final evidence
> Lay in perceptions or in common sense?

When he finds that 'My cause lay in the will' he is able to remake the world of objects in his own egocentric image. Objects are now *his* objects. The world is different because 'my being there is different'. This metaphor reappears in 'The Corridor'.

Several of the poems betray a certain amount of self-pity. It is an existential axiom that man is born free with only himself to rely on, but Gunn manages to make it sound slightly pathetic: 'I am condemned to be/An individual'. This is not the only jarring note in 'Human Condition' for Gunn goes so far as to claim that his own quest for an identity is globally significant:

> I seek, to break, my span.
> I am my one touchstone.
> This is a test more hard
> Than any ever known.
> And thus I keep my guard
> On that which makes me man.

'A Plan of Self Subjection' becomes equally histrionic when he admits that 'As Alexander or Mark Antony/Or Coriolanus, whom I most admire,/I mask self-flattery'. In 'Legal Reform' he runs the whole gamut of self-pity, ending with a privileged and enjoyable despair at being

> Condemned to hope, to happiness, to life,
> Condemned to shift in your enclosing eyes.

Still, he has a future before him and it is a future pregnant with choice. So the book ends fairly optimistically with a poem written in syllabics, 'Vox Humana'. Heavy reliance on the iambic pentameter and metrics generally had driven Gunn into a poetry of effortless slickness where he is not so much imposing form on his thought but letting his thought conform to the exigencies of the metre. In 'Vox Humana' Gunn retains a rhyme scheme of *a b c c b a* (though the rhymes are wildly approximate: *quality/perceive me, first/almost* and so on, and uses seven syllables to the line. This results in more conversational fluency than Gunn hitherto achieved. The speaker in 'Vox Humana' is Choice personified, a 'Being without quality'. Mr Choice offers the individual a welter of opportunity, Mr Choice offers 'All/there is, ever, of future'. Gunn believes that man has nothing to lose but his conceptual chains yet personally has to struggle definitely to make up his mind. 'Vox Humana' neatly concludes *The Sense of Movement*, being fluid and open-ended, closing as it does on the word 'future'.

Gunn's immediate poetic future was settled by the publication, in September 1961, of *My Sad Captains*. The book is stylistically split down the middle. Of the twenty-nine poems, sixteen are written in the slick, assured metrical style hitherto favoured by Gunn. The second part of the book contains thirteen poems written in syllabics, though there is a retention of rhyme as a concession to tradition. As he said later,

> In 1961 I published *My Sad Captains* which is in two
> parts. The first half is the culmination of my old style—
> metrical, rational, but maybe starting to get a little
> more humane. The second half consists of a taking up of
> that humaner impulse in a series of syllabic poems which
> were something new in my work. Syllabics were really
> only a way of teaching myself to write free verse.[12]

12 Autobiographical note written for Faber & Faber, November 1972.

This is an interesting statement. Though Gunn permits an arrogant, potentially powerful, personality to hover over his work, his approach to poetic experiment has been cautious, even timid. In an era when most poets plunge straight into the deep-end of free verse before they have learned to swim in the shallows of rudimentary metrics Gunn shows a genuine humility in his approach to what Dylan Thomas called the 'craft or sullen art' of verse.

Gunn prefaces the first part of *My Sad Captains* with a quotation from Shakespeare's *Troilus and Cressida*: 'The will is infinite and the execution confined, the desire is boundless and the act a slave to limit'. This leads us to expect Gunn to stick to his volitional guns. Instead, the opening poem of the book, 'In Santa Maria del Popolo', turns out to be a most tender and compassionate comment on the predicament of poor people, inspired by a startlingly dramatic painting executed by the sort of man we would expect Gunn to worship. Indeed the life of Michelangelo da Caravaggio would make a splendid subject for a poem in Gunn's early manner. In 1605 he was forced to flee from Rome after wounding a notary, in 1606 he murdered one Rannuccio Tommasoni, in 1609 he himself was wounded, and in 1610 he died alone, stricken by malaria, on the beach of Porto Ercole near Grosseto. A man of violent action if ever there was one. Yet amidst all this frenetic activity Caravaggio found time to paint a series of profoundly original masterpieces like 'The Conversion of St. Paul', 'The Supper at Emmaus', and 'Death of the Virgin'. He was an innovator, a painter whose use of chiaroscuro and dramatic foreshortening made his compositions seem larger than life. Without his stylistic innovations it is unlikely that Rembrandt's art would have taken the direction it did.

So the stage is set for a poem in Gunn's most grand heroic manner, for the painting he chooses to write about is 'The Conversion of St. Paul' which hangs with 'The Crucifixion of St. Peter' in the Cerasi Chapel in the Church of Santa Maria del Popolo in Rome. The painting shows Paul prostrate before his horse, his arms outstretched towards heaven as he embraces his new faith. In *Fighting Terms* there is a sonnet, 'Lerici', which approves of such a dramatic gesture as an emblem for positive action:

> Others make gestures with arms open wide,
> Compressing in the minute before death,

35

> What great expense of muscle and of breath
> They would have made if they had never died.

Instead of repeating his admiration for such a gesture Gunn is content to let the meaning of the painting sweep over him. He is standing in the chapel watching the real shadows mixing with Caravaggio's simulated shadows. It is so gloomy that 'the very subject is in doubt'. Then he sees:

> But evening gives the act, beneath the horse
> And one indifferent groom, I see him sprawl,
> Foreshortened from the head, with hidden face,
> Where he has fallen, Saul becoming Paul.
> O wily painter, limiting the scene
> From a cacophony of dusty forms
> To the one convulsion, what is it you mean
> In that wide gesture of the lifting arms?

At one time Gunn would have answered patly: impulsive action. Now he is not so sure:

> I turn, hardly enlightened, from the chapel
> To the dim interior of the church instead,
> In which there kneel already several people,
> Mostly old women: each head closeted
> In tiny fists holds comfort as it can.
> Their poor arms are too tired for more than this
> —For the large gesture of solitary man,
> Resisting, by embracing, nothingness.

For the first time Gunn has placed the big dramatic gesture in human perspective by admitting to his poetry tired, disillusioned, poor, ignorant, old human beings. At last, Gunn sees that a life of unlimited choice and demonstrative will is only possible for a privileged few who do not have to cope with the physical oppression of poverty and cultural underprivilege. Dramatic gestures are merely a pose. The real human condition is, for the majority, a more tragic experience. For nothing these old women can do in the way of gesture could liberate them from a life tied to a squalid environment. As Gunn himself put it: 'Here at last I begin some kind of critique of the Heroic'.[13]

Tired of mere gestures Gunn turns to 'The Annihilation of Nothing'. Rochester's poem 'Upon Nothing' plays on the notion that something must have preceded creation and that that something was Nothing:

> Nothing thou Elder Brother ev'n to shade,
> Thou hadst a Being e're the World was made,
> And (well fixt) are alone of ending not afraid.

Rochester is, however, merely making fun of a linguistic paradox: in naming Nothing we create a positive concept. To Rochester's generation the universe was created suddenly out of Nothing. To Gunn's generation—the Cambridge generation—the astronomical orthodoxy was continuous creation: the universe has always existed and always will. Man's dread of negativity, of total oblivion comes from his fallacious belief that there is a vacuum waiting to swallow him up. To Gunn, death is merely extinction of the will because even in death the body is organically prolonged. Taking Rochester's paradox to its illogical conclusion Gunn points out that Nothing is full of matter—gas condensing into stars, hydrogen becoming helium—waiting to be shaped by the will. Deploying terza rima with ease and skill Gunn states his case:

> The power that I envisaged, that presided
> Ultimate in its abstract devastations,
> Is merely change, the atoms it divided
>
> Complete, in ignorance, new combinations.
> Only an infinite finitude I see
> In those peculiar lovely variations.

So Gunn has no 'despair that nothing cannot be'. In the 'huge contagious absence' of space there is a universe beyond the physical reach of man but within his mental grasp. Because 'Purposeless matter hovers in the dark' man is able to shoot out concepts and even physical manifestations of them (space probes, for instance).

13 Letter, 7 October 1972.

Having come to terms with meaningless gestures, Gunn has now accepted the intellect as a help not a hindrance.

Having annihilated Nothing Gunn extends his philosophical horizons by inventing his own myth about the origins of conceptual thinking. On a purely narrative level 'The Byrnies'—*byrnies* is the Old English word for chainmail shirts—is about a band of ignorant, blunt-faced, chainmailed heroes afraid of what might lurk unknown in the 'Barbaric forest' they approach. They are afraid of what they do not know, terrified by their own ignorance. In poems like 'For a Birthday' (*Fighting Terms*) Gunn longed to reach a state of preconceptual thinking. Now he sees that such a state has its own terrors. In order to relate himself to the world man—even if that man be a byrnie—must be able to classify the unfamiliar. Otherwise knowledge would be impossible, man would be a purely instinctive animal. Man must relate each object to a general concept of that object. Each tree is a particular example of a conceptual tree, each man is an example of the species Man. In 'The Byrnies' Gunn calls the concept 'the constant Thing' against which objects must be tested. The Byrnies see a vast chaotic forest on which sunlight dances. They are puzzled by the way the objects are transformed as light passes over them. They do not know if these objects are undergoing permanent change or are simply appearing to change. Then when they see sunlight trapped in their own familiar chainmail they realise that the objects they see are real objects trapping the light:

> Thus for each blunt-faced ignorant one
> The great grey rigid uniform combined
>   Safety with virtue of the sun.
> Thus concepts linked like chainmail in the mind.

The Byrnies are heroes, we are told in the first line of the poem. They are also soldiers. These two concepts seem linked like chainmail in Thom Gunn's mind. The soldier seems to typify for Gunn the one member of society who can act like an animal without having to suffer mental agony over violent acts because his are sanctified by society. Neither does the soldier have to conduct a heart-searching search for an identity: he puts one on with his uniform. He has a role and a precise function, just like an animal. In his first two books Gunn has been anxious to show that civilised man is burdened by his consciousness of received moral laws and tradition. The soldier has no such doubts—not when he is in uniform anyway. However, *My Sad Captains* is in some ways a book in which Gunn expiates for the sins of discipline and will committed in *Fighting Terms* and *The Sense of Movement*. So he is willing to criticise the purpose and will and lack of cultural consciousness of the soldier.

The soldier in 'Innocence' is a true professional. The sum-total of his knowledge is 'The egotism of a healthy body'. He is innocently ignorant of the past, that 'Culture of guilt and guilt's vague heritage,/Self-pity and the soul'. He is, therefore, as unlike Gunn as it is possible to be. Yet opposites attract and the soldier has a fascination for Gunn:

> The Corps developed, it was plain to see,
> Courage, endurance, loyalty and skill
> To a morale firm as morality,
> Hardening him to an instrument.

So though the soldier has the 'part solution' of the Boys of 'On the Move'—courage allied to a firm morale—Gunn acknowledges that this part solution is merely irresponsibility. For the soldier is not deliberately cruel; he is simply carrying out instructions with a genuine innocence of the point of view of the person designated as enemy. The death of another human being does not evoke even a trace of humanity:

> When he stood near the Russian partisan
> Being burned alive, he therefore could behold
> The ribs wear gently through the darkening skin
> And sicken only at the Northern cold.

Gun has said of 'Innocence', 'I'm trying to show how the celebration of energy can lead one to a kind of commitment where one finds that energy is not just a vacuum; it is very often destroying the energy of other people and is therefore maybe not such a great energy.'[14] It is a credit to Gunn that he has been able to question the attitudes of his earlier work so radically.

There remains one professional soldier for whom Gunn has an unqualified admiration: Claus von Stauffenberg. Unlike the soldier in 'Innocence', von Stauffenberg is presented as a soldier who has not forgotten his sense of honour. It is worth reminding oneself exactly who this Gunnian hero is since in 'Claus von Stauffenberg' Gunn glosses him simply as 'of the bomb-plot on Hitler, 1944'. Count von Stauffenberg was a German officer who had lost his right hand, two fingers of his left hand, and his left eye in combat in Tunisia. As a soldier he had carried out orders issued by the Nazi state. Gunn says he had 'two remaining fingers and a will', but it is more likely that it was his submission to Nazism that allowed him access to Hitler, because Hitler normally avoided the Prussian aristocracy like the plague. On 20 July 1944 von Stauffenberg placed a brief-case packed with plastic explosive in Hitler's hut in Rastenburg. Taking advantage of the bomb's ten-minute fuse the 'maimed young Colonel', as Gunn calls him, headed for his waiting plane and took off after the explosion. He was thus cut off from his fellow conspirators in Berlin, unable to tell them that Hitler had survived the blast. Not only was the attempt on Hitler's life a failure but von Stauffenberg's own motives do not bear much examination. By waiting until 1944 to oppose Hitler it seems that his plan was more to save his beloved Germany from imminent defeat rather than to liberate the world from Nazism.

As a result of his action Hitler's security was tightened and the Fuehrer had a new lease of life. As a further result of the abortive attempt on Hitler's life

> Everybody in Germany who bore the name of Stauffen-
> berg, men, women and children, many of them very
> distant cousins who in some cases had never even met
> Claus von Stauffenberg, were arrested. 'The family of
> Count Stauffenberg', Himmler said at Posen, 'will be
> wiped out root and branch', and indeed many members
> of it died in the camps.[15]

14 *London Magazine*, November 1964, p. 67.
15 Constantine Fitzgibbon, *To Kill Hitler*, London (Tom Stacey) 1972, p. 220.

Stauffenberg, mutilated and fearful for the future of his fatherland, had little to live for and died before a firing squad shouting 'Long live free Germany'. Yet Gunn eulogises this Nazi officer as 'The rational man' and dedicates this quatrain to him:

> And though he fails, honour personified
> In a cold time where honour cannot grow,
> He stiffens, like a statue, in mid-stride
> —Falling toward history, and under snow.

Not only is the fundamental image plagiarised from Ted Hughes's 'Bayonet Charge' (*The Hawk in the Rain*) where the soldier's 'foot hung like a statuary in mid-stride', but to call such a man as Claus von Stauffenberg 'honour personified' is politically naive. There are more candidates for heroism among the multitude of men who opposed Hitler from his beginning. Gunn is unable, in this poem, to see past the heroic gesture. His sympathy would have been better directed towards those who suffered as a result of von Stauffenberg's blunders.

If the Nazi movement is at least as dead as von Stauffenberg its uniform survives as an identity substitute. The gear reappears in *My Sad Captains* in 'Black Jackets' which is vintage Gunn: the inarticulate in search of an identity. The poem describes a red-haired van-driver bored out of his mind with his repetitive job, anonymously dressed all week in overalls. Gunn suggests that it is the military glamour of motorbike gear that attracts individuals like this red-haired boy. In ordinary clothes they are nothing and feel nothing. Once they put on the leather-jacket uniform they appear instantly aggressive and exude a sense of menace. The boy has come to a regular meeting place with others exactly like himself, where he can feel a sense of belonging. The red-haired van-driver, ignorantly existential in the sense that 'The present was the things he stayed among', submerges his inconsequential conventional upbringing in the gang mentality:

> If it was only loss he wore,
> He wore it to assert, with fierce devotion,
> Complicity and nothing more.
> He recollected his initiation,

> And one especially of the rites.
> For on his shoulders they had put tatoos:
> The group's name on the left, The Knights,
> And on the right the slogan Born to Lose.

Gunn has at least the humanity to see that beneath the fierce leather exterior there lurks a rather pathetic red-haired van-boy.

Another pathetic hero appears in the first of two poems called 'Modes of Pleasure'. Here we have a man of sexual action, a man who has lived by his will (and it is worth pointing out that in the Elizabethen age 'will' was a frequent euphemism for the male sexual organ) becoming old, 'fallen from/The heights of twenty to middle age'. Having 'used each hour of leisure/To learn by rote the modes of pleasure' he has no past to console him, only a series of staccato sexual encounters. They have not enhanced him in any way, not extended his consciousness. The soldier in 'Incident on a Journey' (*Fighting Terms*) said 'I acted, and my action made me wise'. The 'Fallen Rake' in 'Modes of Pleasure' knows better:

> He knows that nothing, not the most
> Cunning or sweet, can hold him, still.
> Living by habit of the will,
> He cannot contemplate the past.

All the man of sexual action can do is wait while 'The will awaits its gradual end'. The second 'Modes of Pleasure' poem presents the point of view of the Rake before his Fall. It is a cynical address to a woman he plans to conquer. Bluntly he asks 'Why pretend/Love must accompany erection?' However, even phallic pride has its fall, as we know from the previous poem.

Just as 'In Praise of Cities' was the most deeply-felt love-poem in *The Sense of Movement*, so is 'A Map of the City'—with the massive exception of 'In Santa Maria del Popolo'—the most poignant poem in the first half of *My Sad Captains*. For Gunn sees best at a distance, he prefers humans in general to particular human beings.

> I stand upon a hill and see
> A luminous country under me,

> Through which at two the drunk must weave;
> The transient's pause, the sailor's leave.

This Olympian attitude is reversed in 'The Value of Gold' where, lying flat out with his head on the grass, Gunn becomes 'insect size' to contemplate the purpose of growth that goes on without human intervention. He is, in fact, irrelevant to the progress of nature.

It is in this mood of humility that Gunn writes 'Considering the Snail'. This poem belongs to the second half of *My Sad Captains*, the syllabics half. He uses seven syllables to the line with an approximate rhyme-scheme of *a b c a b c*. Whereas up to now Gunn had considered the grand gestures of heroic men, now he turns to a conventionally unattractive creature, the snail, and dignifies it with this beautifully exact description:

> The snail pushes through a green
> night, for the grass is heavy
> with water and meets over
> the bright path he makes, where rain
> has darkened the earth's dark.

For once, Gunn refrains from drawing a large conclusion about the creature he has observed. He is content to make the reader a present of this particular snail that has kept its foot on the ground instead of slavering through Gunn's egocentric brain cells. He admits 'I cannot tell/what power is at work, drenched there/with purpose, knowing nothing'. He is, however, convinced that the one-dimensional world of the snail takes in the 'slow passion/to that deliberate progress'. The poem itself is something of a progression for Gunn in that he has shown himself capable of caring about something so utterly unlike himself.

'Considering the Snail' is the showpiece of the syllabic half of *My Sad Captains*. Apart from the closing poem of the book, the others are basically exercises in syllabics, exercises that allow Gunn to begin to respond to nature, to see nature without the intervention of his self.

Up to now his heroes have been people he read about. People like Albert Camus, Claus von Stauffenberg, Stendhal, Shakespeare. In the title poem of the book he says:

> They were men
> who, I thought, lived only to
> renew the wasteful force they
> spent with each hot convulsion.

Gunn, however, is ready to say Goodbye to all That. The title of
the poem, and the collection as a whole, is derived appropriately
enough from Shakespeare's *Antony and Cleopatra*. Appropriate
because Mark Antony (see 'A Plan of Self Subjection', *The Sense
of Movement*) is as much a hero to Gunn as Shakespeare is, and it
is Antony who says

> Come,
> Let's have one other gaudy night: call to me
> All my sad captains, fill our bowls: once more
> Let's mock the midnight bell

> (III. xiii. 182–5)

Gunn has little use now for 'disinterested/hard energy' and so he
watches as his sad captains, his heroic men of intellectual and
physical action, 'withdraw to an orbit'. Gunn has called this
closing piece 'A good sad serious poem that rounds off this part of
my poetry, poetry in much of which I emphasise the will as an end
in itself. From now on, a bit more flexibility.'[16]

16 Letter, 7 October 1972.

3   'No Falsifying Dream'

When *The Hawk in the Rain* appeared in September 1957 Ted Hughes was in the USA with his American wife, Sylvia Plath. They had gone to Northampton, Massachusetts, so that Sylvia could teach freshman English at Smith College and Ted take creative writing and literary courses at the University of Massachusetts. To complete the American ambiance *The Hawk in the Rain* was chosen to receive the First Publication Award in a contest judged by W.H. Auden, Stephen Spender and Marianne Moore and conducted by the New York Poetry Center of the Young Men's and Young Women's Hebrew Association in co-operation with New York publishers Harper & Brothers. However, the poems in *The Hawk in the Rain* were not fashionably American-orientated or even cosmopolitan. They were deeply rooted in the West Riding of Yorkshire. They displayed a countryman's love-hatred of the soil, they showed a keen appreciation of the weather as a guide to the temper of nature.

It was evident in the first stanza of the first poem, the title poem, of the book:

> I drown in the drumming ploughland, I drag up
> Heel after heel from the swallowing of the earth's mouth,
> From clay that clutches my each step to the ankle
> With the habit of the dogged grave, but the hawk . . . .

It was there in 'Wind', the poem Hughes wrote about his parents' house 'The Beacon' in Heptonstall Slack:

> At noon I scaled along the house-side as far as
> The coal-house door. I dared once to look up—
> Through the brunt wind that dented the balls of my eyes
> The tent of the hills drummed and strained its guyrope.

It was there in his determination, expressed in 'The Horses', to keep his roots in the West Riding, even amidst modern cities and crowds and the passing of time. Such moments represented the quintessential Hughes, the man accustomed to reflecting on human life from the heights of the Yorkshire moors. He, as a poet, would stand on the highest hill among the elements, responding to animal life: the activities of human beings would be something that went on in the valleys he saw from a god's perspective.

The Hawk in the Rain, dedicated 'To Sylvia' who had been his wife for fifteen months in September 1957, contained forty poems, the longest of which, 'Six Young Men', contained only 45 lines. So the book was a series of beginnings, short observations and meditations, not a sustained vision of an imaginative world. It is therefore somewhat erratic, displaying Hughes's strengths and weaknesses in a rather obvious way. The poet was 27, no precocious infant of genius. He was a youngish man in no particular hurry. In fact in the best of the poems there was an attempt at timelessness, the sort of timelessness a man might experience on lonely hills where 'the horizons endure', and in the greatest of the poems a timelessness solidly communicated. It is as well to establish at the outset the themes that Hughes was interested in exploring for they have not really changed with the passing of time, only intensified.

The book is arranged in bunches of thematically linked items after this fashion:

ANIMAL POEMS: 'The Hawk in the Rain', 'The Jaguar', 'Macaw and Little Miss', 'The Thought Fox', 'The Horses'

INTERLUDE: 'Famous Poet'

LOVE AND SEX: 'Song', 'Parlour Piece', 'Secretary', 'Soliloquy of a Misanthrope', 'The Dove Breeder', 'Billet-Doux', 'A Modest Proposal', 'Incompatibilities', 'September', 'Fall-grief's Girl-Friends', 'Two Phases', 'The Decay of Vanity', 'Fair Choice', 'The Conversion of the Reverend Skinner', 'Complaint'

INTELLECTUALS: 'Phaetons', 'Egg-Head', 'The Man Seeking Experience Enquires His Way of a Drop of Water', 'Meeting'

ELEMENTS: 'Wind', 'October Dawn'

DEATH: 'Roarers in a Ring', 'Vampire', 'Childbirth', 'The Hag', 'Law in the Country of the Cats', 'Invitation to the Dance'

WAR: 'The Casualty', 'Bayonet Charge', 'Griefs for Dead Soldiers', 'Six Young Men', 'Two Wise Generals', 'The Ancient Heroes and the Bomber Pilot'

FINALE: 'The Martyrdom of Bishop Farrar'.

Hughes emerges from this arrangement as a man with a respect for the force of nature and a contempt for the aspirations of man.

Stylistically the biggest influence on the book is Dylan Thomas. Hughes has said 'As for Thomas, *Deaths and Entrances* was a holy book with me for quite a time when it first came out'.[1] What Hughes took from Thomas was a pulsating verbal energy, a vision of death in life, an emphasis on blood and bone and a hyperbolic imagery.

Thomas himself drew on the precedent of Gerard Manley Hopkins for his exuberance and Hughes has clearly found Hopkins' Sprung Rhythm a theoretical justification for language rooted in West Riding speech. Hughes prefers monosyllabic stress to iambic accents and would surely have agreed with Hopkins that Sprung Rhythm is 'the rhythm of common speech and of written prose, when rhythm is perceived in them'.[2]

It is the profound echo of Dylan Thomas that is heard in Hughes's 'The Hawk in the Rain'—specifically Thomas's 'Over Sir John's hill'. Hughes has 'the hawk/Effortlessly at height hangs his still eye', 'the hawk hangs/The diamond point of will', 'the hawk hangs still'. Thomas has 'The hawk on fire hangs still', 'The hawk on fire, the halter height', 'the hawk on fire in hawk-eyed dusk'. Thomas's hawk is a gallows. Hughes's hawk is all hawk: a killer whose 'wings hold all creation in a weightless quiet'.

Hughes believes that the strength of animals lies in their instinct and precise function: 'Animals are not violent, they're so much more completely controlled than men. So much more adapted to their environment.'[3] So while the poet is almost swallowed up by

1 *London Magazine*, January 1961, p. 12.
2 G.M. Hopkins, 'Author's Preface' c.1883, reprinted in *Gerard Manley Hopkins*, ed. W.H. Gardner, Harmondsworth (Penguin Books) 1953, p. 11.
3 *The Guardian*, 23 March 1965, p. 9.

mud, mastered by this earthy element the hawk 'Effortlessly at height hangs his still eye'. While the ferocious wind

> Thumbs my eyes, throws my breath, tackles my heart,
> And rain hacks my head to the bone, the hawk hangs
> The diamond point of will that polestars
> The sea drowner's endurance.

This is a radical note in nature poetry. Previous celebrants of nature have, like Gerard Manley Hopkins, marvelled at the variety and beauty of animals; or, like D.H. Lawrence, seen them as analogous to man. Hughes, however, deliberately puts man at a disadvantage compared with animals. In this poem he exists on a lower earth-bound level than the hawk. For Hughes, animals are pure embodied function. They are not, like man, vitiated by spurious morality or incapacitated by doubt. A hawk is a hawk whereas a man has ambitions to be God-like and is thus permanently frustrated. The hawk is forever in its own element even when it dies an elemental death as it 'meets the weather/Coming the wrong way'.

From an animal in its own element Hughes turns to an animal caged by man. To Hughes, zoos are prisons where animals are condemned to solitary confinement for the crime of being non-human. They are put behind bars as if to prove man's mastery over the other species. However, as 'The Jaguar' suggests, man cannot cage in animal energy and instinct, especially that of the jaguar. It is a sunny day at the zoo and tiger and lion and boa-constrictor laze in the heat:

> But who runs like the rest past these arrives
> At a cage where the crowd stands, stares, mesmerized,
> As a child at a dream, at a jaguar hurrying enraged
> Through prison darkness after the drills of his eyes.

The jaguar's instinct cannot be extinguished, its genetic inheritance is of whole-hearted jaguar-ness, it has 'the bang of blood in the brain'. Its essence is summed up in its being. It is. Man tries to be something. Even in his man-made cage the jaguar remains true to itself.

In 'Macaw and Little Miss' Hughes makes a poem out of the antithesis between human frustration and instinctive animal energy. The setting is contrived to derive the maximum contrast between the pathetic fustiness of a 'civilised' old lady—what energy there was exhausted in maturity—and the primitive uncageable burning energy of the bird.

The point is as subtle as a sore thumb: humans are more caged in their domestic environment than animals are in their cages. Like the aspidistra the old woman 'succumbs/To the musk of faded velvet'. The macaw retains its instinct. This point is not lost on the old lady's grand-daughter who is not yet old enough to have entirely succumbed to domestic dust. She still has her dreams:

> The dream where the warrior comes, lightning and iron,
> Smashing and burning and rending towards her loin:
> > Deep into her pillow her silence pleads.

Given the stifling claustrophobic sterility of the domestic human condition nothing corresponds to her dream so much as the macaw whom she tries to seduce with sweet talk, whispers and kisses. Yet she cannot possess his energy and in an excess of frustration she 'strikes the cage in a tantrum and swirls out' while the bird explodes in 'conflagration and frenzy,/And his shriek shakes the house.'

In Hughes's world the only way to come to terms with the animals is not to tame them, but to become possessed by them, which is precisely what happens in 'The Thought-Fox', probably the finest of the five animal poems in *The Hawk in the Rain.* Talking about his childhood passion for capturing animals Hughes has described the composition of the poem:

> An animal I never succeeded in keeping alive is the fox. I was always frustrated: twice by a farmer, who killed cubs I had caught before I could get to them, and once by a poultry keeper who freed my cub while his dog waited. Years after those events I was sitting up late one snowy night in dreary lodgings in London. I had written nothing for a year or so but that night I got the idea I might write something and I wrote in a few

minutes 'The Thought-Fox': the first 'animal' poem I ever wrote.[4]

If we compare this poem with Thom Gunn's 'Allegory of the Wolf Boy' (*The Sense of Movement*) we will see a significant difference. Gunn, like most poets who perceive the animal part of man, offers a distant allegorical detached situation for our edification. Hughes does not stand in judgement of the animal. He wants its essence to enter into him. For although 'The Thought-Fox' is a fox of the imagination it is presented with a beautifully solid foxy reality.

When the fox does come it is 'Coming about its own business'— functioning as a fox—and is welcomed into the vacuum in the human head, the vacuum created when instinct had to vacate a place for excessive cerebration:

> Till, with a sudden sharp hot stink of fox
> It enters the dark hole of the head.

Making a foxhole out of the human brain reveals how consistently Hughes sardonically dismisses the physical seat of learning. In this case, instinct replaces intellect. In his verbal re-creation of the fox Hughes disdains strict rhyme and iambic pentameter. These tradition-worn artefacts would have frightened the fox away. Hughes's rhythm is mimetic, seeking to simulate the action of the poem. The monosyllables in those memorable lines—

> Till, with a sudden sharp hot stink of fox
> It enters the dark hole of the head—

really do suggest the movement of the fox as it approaches the safety of the metaphorical foxhole. There is the swift, sudden little trot ('with a sudden'), then the cautious careful tread ('sharp hot stink of fox'), then the confident measured pace ('the dark hole of the head'). It is a remarkable gift for embodying words with animal rhythm.

'The Horses' is composed in free couplets, most of which end solidly on nouns: 'bird', 'wood', 'light', 'horses', 'hooves', 'head', 'ridge', 'sun', 'cloud'. This places the emphasis on the physical

4 *Poetry in the Making*, London (Faber & Faber) 1967, p. 19.

presence of the natural elements that constitute the horses' environment. The narrative content of the poem is slight. In the dark hour before dawn the poet climbs through the woods onto the frozen moors. The ten horses make no acknowledgment of his presence, they are timeless: 'Megalith-still . . . making no move'. They inhabit their own world, they are 'Grey silent fragments/ Of a grey silent world' (evidence that Hughes, like Gunn, has profitably read Edwin Muir, whose creatures in his own poem 'The Horses' were 'Dropped in some wilderness of the broken world'). Hughes compares his own inability to cope with the elements—'I listened in emptiness on the moor-ridge', 'I turned/Stumbling in the fever of a dream'—to the horses' relationship with nature. The eruption of the sun onto the moors disturbs Hughes but not the horses:

> There, still they stood,
> But now steaming and glistening under the flow of light.

The horses are as 'patient as the horizons'. They endure.

Hughes makes a credo out of the example of the horses. Like them, he wants to inhabit a timeless world and be tested by the elements. Yeat's ideal was 'a small cabin . . . of clay and wattles made' on the Isle of Innisfree, a haven of peace to which he could escape from the squalor of the city. Ted Hughes chooses instead the disturbing solitude of the Yorkshire moors:

> In din of the crowded streets, going among the years, the
> faces,
> May I still meet my memory in so lonely a place
>
> Between the streams and the red clouds, hearing curlews,
> Hearing the horizons endure.

It could be a poet like Yeats whom Hughes describes in 'Famous Poet'.* While Hughes reveres the poetry of Yeats he must have questioned the propriety of this monstrously arrogant, egotistical, supercilious, sexually obsessed, selfish beast lurking in the poet's

*Ted Hughes has pointed out that he had the Polish poet, Mizkiewitz in mind – not Yeats.

clothing. So Hughes's famous poet has 'the demeanour of a mouse,/ Yet he is a monster'. He is monstrous because he has outlived his vitality. All he can do is repeat early triumphs, feebly attempt tricks he performed so well in his youth. For Hughes, 'Poetry is not made out of thoughts or casual fancies. It is made out of experiences which change our bodies, and spirits, whether momentarily or for good'.[5] This famous poet is no longer capable of such experiences, his talent has atrophied with his body. His efforts at repeat performances have 'left him wrecked'. He is a living fossil, like a Stegosaurus (the dinosaur with a brain at one end and a brain at the other in order that together they might cope with the dead weight in between). It is people like him, instinct gone, that should be 'set/To blink behind bars at the zoo'—not jaguars.

Hughes is nothing if not thematically persistent and having introduced us to the notion of the domestic cage in 'Macaw and Little Miss' he keeps it in our minds. 'Parlour Piece' describes a couple of human lovebirds trapped in their domestic cage. Fearful of giving full expression to their feelings they trap their thoughts over 'Pale cool tea in tea-cups'. 'Secretary' concerns a 30-year-old virgin so tamed by her domestic cage—her 'Safe home' where 'She mends socks with holes, shirts that are torn,/For father and mother'—that she is terrified of physical contact with men:

> all
> Day like a starling under the bellies of bulls
> She hurries among men, ducking, peeping.

Hughes has no sympathy for such a denial of life. Indeed, in 'Soliloquy of a Misanthrope', he takes sardonic pleasure in imaging such women as the secretary succumbing to the embrace of the earth in death as they 'grimace/Under the commitments of their flesh'. A more apt title for this poem would surely have been 'Soliloquy of a Misogynist'.

Sex, as Hughes is by no means the first to discover, is the one passion we have in common with the animals. 'The Dove Breeder' looks at sex as a force capable of unmanning a mild-mannered man, making him all animal. Everything the dove breeder has

5 *Ibid*, p. 32.

carefully arranged is shattered when 'Love struck into his life/Like a hawk into a dovecote', so

> Now he rides the morning mist
> With a big-eyed hawk on his fist.

And judging from 'Billet-Doux', a hawkish, predatory woman is an ideal antidote to the intellectual love of indolent procrastination. Such a woman is one

> Who sees straight through bogeyman,
> The crammed cafés, the ten thousand
> Books packed end to end, even my gross bulk.

Left to his own bookish devices the intellectual is prey to the hawk of despair. Better that he should rise from his despair and encounter the creative force that resides in a woman:

> Love's a spoiled appetite for some delicacy—
> I am driven to your bed and four walls
> From bottomlessly breaking night.

The pun on 'delicacy' as both fragility and a tasty morsel contains the two attitudes men normally take to sex. Hughes adds a third view: sex as a physical salvation from intellectual despair.

For it is the intellectual who sums up, for Hughes, the warped evolution of man. Instead of evolving a new role man has refined the basic animal instinct out of himself and put nothing significant in its place. What he is left with is a vestigial animal appetite that is continually at war with his intellect.

In his poems on intellectuals Hughes attempts to put man in his place by exposing his pretensions. It is the contention of the intellectual that he can contain the universe inside his mind. Hughes begs to differ. It is the contention of man that he can tame nature. Again Hughes dissents, believing that man is afraid of nature.

'Egg-Head' is an unambiguous display of disgust at the absurdity of the intellectual 'Peeping through his fingers at the world's ends/Or at an ant's head'. Unable to accept that the outside universe is bigger than his comprehension he 'shuts out the world's

53

knocking/With a welcome', 'resists receiving the flash/Of the sun. the bolt of the earth' and instead draws arrogance from his own ignorance and ends in 'Braggart-browed complacency'. 'The Man Seeking Experience Enquires his Way of a Drop of Water' presents an absurd academic philosopher attempting to see a world in a drop of water on his kitchen wall. Hughes ridicules this man by putting in his mouth a ludicrously grandiloquent address to the drop of water ('Having studied a journey in the high/Cathedralled brain, the mole's ear...') and then equating it with 'baby-talk'. For 'This droplet was clear simple water still' after all the intellectual's words have been spilled on it.

To me such poems about intellectuals fail because Hughes protests too much. Fearful of being considered an intellectual himself he indulges in a frenzy of dissociation and ends up too close for comfort to the object of his attack. They are purely negative poems. Hughes is much better in his own element: the world of nature. It is then that he speaks for himself, speaks in a broad accent of rough justice imposed on man by the elements. Hughes's ideal poetic idiom seems to be:

> A utility general-purpose style, as, for instance, Shakespeare's was, that combines a colloquial prose readiness with poetic breadth, a ritual intensity and music of an exceedingly high order with clear direct feeling, and yet in the end is nothing but casual speech.[6]

He achieves this ideal in the magnificent poem 'Wind' which is one of the most memorable moments of *The Hawk in the Rain*.

'Wind' takes as its physical starting point his parents' house 'The Beacon'. It is, as I discovered when trying to find it in order to have a word with Ted's father, Bill Hughes, 'the big house with the green windows'. Hughes, more poetically, described it as 'some fine green goblet'. The poem is full of superbly physical images that transform so-called ordinary objects into objects of wonder. The house itself is compared to a ship at sea:

> This house has been far out at sea all night,
> The woods crashing through darkness, the booming hills,

6 Hughes, *Selected Poems of Keith Douglas*, London (Faber & Faber) 1964, p. 14.

Winds stampeding the fields under the window
Floundering black astride and blinding wet.

The light is 'like the lens of a mad eye', 'the skyline a grimace',
'a black-/Back gull bent like an iron bar slowly'. What comes
crashing through this welter of imagery is the sense of the fragility
of people menaced by the elements, on the point of being overwhelmed by them. On the subject of this poem Hughes has said:

> On and off I live in a house on top of a hill in the
> Pennines, where the wind blows without obstruction
> across the tops of the moors. I have experienced some
> gales in that house, and ['Wind'] is a poem I once
> wrote about one of them....In writing that poem I was
> mainly concerned with the strength of the blast, the
> way it seems to shake the world up like a box of toys.[7]

Hughes's poetic world is anything but anthropocentric. Rather
his images orbit the prehistoric world when man was a creature
among creatures, an animal battling for survival. As a result of
this obsession with the dark mysterious world of the past, Hughes
feels that the modern world does not constitute a big enough
challenge and he constantly invokes the prehistoric past. 'October
Dawn' takes place the morning after the night before. There has
been a party on the lawn and the poem begins with an observation:

> October is marigold, and yet
> A glass half full of wine left out
>
> To the dark heaven all night, by dawn
> Has dreamed a premonition
>
> Of ice across its eye as if
> The ice-age had begun its heave.

The ice-age is the era when the mammoth inexplicably froze
into extinction. Hughes wants to give them a second chance,
another ice-age when

---

7 Hughes, *Poetry in the Making*, London (Faber & Faber) 1970, p. 33.

>   sound by sight
>   Will Mammoth and Sabre-tooth celebrate
>
>   Reunion while a fist of cold
>   Squeezes the fire at the core of the world,
>
>   Squeezes the fire at the core of the heart,
>   And now it is about to start.

These couplets are an invocation to a chaotic past. Hughes feels that the mammoth is massive enough to put man in his place, remind him of his puny part in the evolutionary process. It is a persistent image representing the energy that man's frigid intellectuality civilised out of existence. For example:

>   Columbus' huckstering breath
>   Blew inland through North America
>
>   Killing the last of the mammoths.
>   ('Fourth of July', *Lupercal*)
>
>
>   The tight-vest lamb
>   With its wriggle eel tail
>   and its wintry eye
>   With its ice-age mammoth
>   unconcern
>   Letting the aeon
>   seconds go by.
>   ('New Year Song', *Spring Summer Autumn Winter*)
>
>
>   Moonlight freezes the shaggy world
>   Like a mammoth of ice—
>   The past and the future
>   Are the jaws of a steel vice.
>   ('The Warm and the Cold', *Spring Summer Autumn
>   Winter*)

'Roarers in a Ring' is a poem that begins with the trivial sound of a Christmas carol ('Snow fell as for Wenceslas' instead of the syllabically similar 'Good King Wenceslas looked out') before being dramatically transformed into a tragic ballad:

> The air was new as a razor,
>   The moor looked like the moon,
> When they all went roaring homewards
>   An hour before dawn.

(The hour before dawn is for Hughes the time when humans sleep and animals come into their own, cf. 'the hour-before-dawn dark' in 'The Horses'.) It is Christmas Eve and a group of drunken farmers celebrate the birth of Christ by drinking themselves into a mindlessly hearty laughter. Yet Hughes would not be Hughes if he did not see some cosmic significance in the furious despair-drowning drinking of the farmers. For them the birth of Christ has not affected the fall of man, for on this Christmas Eve they still fall foul of their own natures, thud down to the ground

> While the world under their footsoles
>   Went whirling still
> Gay and forever, in the bottomless black
>   Silence through which it fell.

War is a theme that has fascinated Hughes to the point of obsession. He was nine when World War Two began, and had recently moved, with his family, to Mexborough in south Yorkshire. At Mexborough Grammar School Hughes must have taken a keen schoolboy interest in the war and seen it, like most schoolboys, through the rosy spectacles of official patriotic propaganda. As a result, it made little impression on him. Instead it was World War One that made the biggest impact on Hughes. He relived it as he sat at his father's feet and heard tales of Gallipoli and massacres and young men going to die. Hughes has said that 'most poetry is not equipped for life in a world where people actually do die. But some is'.[8] Hughes is determined that his poetry will acknowledge death.

As a result of this determination the war poems in *The Hawk in the Rain* are, with the animal poems, the most deeply-felt pieces in the book. War makes man live in the shadow of death where there is room only for essentials, not trivialities. In 'The

---

8 Hughes, introduction to *Vasko Popa: Selected Poems*, Harmondsworth (Penguin Books) 1969, pp. 9–10.

Casualty' war is reluctantly acknowledged by the civilian population who live 'behind steamed windows' and whose perspective is defined by 'the washing hung out'. Into this sleepy English town atmosphere war in the shape of a 'burning aircraft' comes like an invasion. Typically the animals are first to acknowledge it. While the people drift along in their lethargy 'a pheasant/Is craning every way in astonishment', a hare 'Flattens ears and tears madly away', 'the wren warns': Icarus-like 'a man fell out of the air alive'. His body contains more physical reality than is possessed by the whole of the civilian population put together: 'the burned man/Bulks closer greater flesh and blood than their own'. It is his death they acknowledge who are unable to grasp the import of life. Death is what they understand and they 'start to the edge/Of such horror close as mourners can,/Greedy to share all that is undergone'.

In war man recovers his animal instinct for survival. 'Bayonet Charge' states this dramatically in the first sentence: 'Suddenly he awoke and was running'. The soldier's mind is so wonderfully concentrated on the fact of staying alive that he has no time for man-made abstract concepts that insult the reality they seek to contain:

> King, honour, human dignity, et cetera
> Dropped like luxuries in a yelling alarm
> To get out of that blue crackling air
> His terror's touchy dynamite.

The reality of death is only apprehended by those it affects as a particular, unique, precise physical fact. This is the point of the three attitudes to death examined in 'Griefs for Dead Soldiers'. The poem is composed in three sections, each of two unrhymed seven-line stanzas. Each stanza gives a different outlook on death. First, the 'mightiest' grief will be the official one, elaborately stagemanaged for the patriotic edification of the civilian population, 'the crowds that know of no other wound'. Second, the 'secretest' grief is the grief of the widow who watches

> The telegram opening of its own accord
> Inescapably and more terribly than any bomb
> That dives to the cellar and lifts the house.

The widow is diminished by this death, she 'cannot build her sorrow into a monument/And walk away from it'. Her world is as smashed as the body of her dead husband. Third, the 'truest' grief is experienced by those who have to bury the dead: other soldiers who give vent to no dramatic tears but accept death as a fact of everyday life:

> The burial party works with a craftsman calm.
> Weighing their grief by the ounce, and burying it.

In 'Six Young Men' Hughes himself experiences a fourth kind of grief: the remotest. He looks at a photograph of six Yorkshiremen who died forty years before. The photograph shows them 'trimmed for a Sunday jaunt', happy and optimistic, yet 'six months after this picture they were all dead'. The Yorkshire landscape has not changed since their deaths, only their absence is conspicuous:

> I know
> That bilberried bank, that thick tree, that black wall,
> Which are here yet and not changed. From where these
> sit
> You hear the water of seven streams fall
> To the roarer in the bottom, and through all
> The leafy valley a rumouring of air go.
> Pictured here, their expressions listen yet,
> And still that valley has not changed its sound
> Though their faces are four decades under the ground.

That beautifully precise description of a particular part of the west Yorkshire landscape puts us in the position of the six young men, and enables Hughes to tell the reader, 'That man's not more alive whom you confront. . . . Than any of these six celluloid smiles are'. Their deaths, though distant, represent more reality than the living will ever imagine because there is 'No thought so vivid as their smoking blood'. The didactic point of the poem is, despite the remarkable act of empathy on Hughes's part, somewhat perverse since no one is, or should, confront death merely as a means of experiencing life more intensely.

'Two Wise Generals' is reminiscent of Siegfried Sassoon's 'The General' which ends:

> 'He's a cheery old card' grunted Harry to Jack
> As they slogged up to Arras with rifle and pack.
>   .   .   .   .   .
> But he did for them both by his plan of attack.

In Hughes's poem there are two such generals. The narrator in 'The Ancient Heroes and the Bomber Pilot' is the bomber pilot himself who finds that his role in war does not match the expectations he assimilated from books. This pilot can destroy cities at the touch of a button yet is nostalgic for the mythical days when war was an adventure, when warriors earned fame 'with fresh sacks-full of heads'. The pernicious romanticism of such a character as the bomber pilot is nauseating, but it would be an insult to attribute such an attitude to Hughes himself: the other war poems are too solidly real for that.

The Hawk in the Rain closes with 'The Martyrdom of Bishop Farrar', about a Protestant burned by Bloody Mary's Roman Catholic fanaticism. In Hughes's version of things the death by burning becomes Bishop Farrar's 'finest hour' (or however long it takes to burn a man). In the eyes of the 'sullen-jowled watching Welsh townspeople' the Bishop's fortitude in the face of burning means more than all his wordy sermons. The Bishop is a hero to Hughes also because he felt his words were worth dying for and so

> out of his eyes,
> Out of his mouth, fire like a glory broke,
> And smoke burned his sermons into the skies.

That is the kind of commitment to words that Hughes, in his heart of hearts, would wish poets to possess.

Lupercal, like *The Hawk in the Rain* dedicated 'To Sylvia', was published in March 1960. It is not so methodically arranged as *The Hawk in the Rain* but the thematic territory is much the same. What Hughes has done, though, is to concentrate on his strengths.

Whereas there were five animal poems in the first volume, there are twelve in the second, and they include the best work in the book. The most famous, the most anthologised of the animal poems—though not necessarily the best—is 'Hawk Roosting'.

The poem begins with the hawk defining its nature. It has its eyes closed but its body is still alive to instinct. It has none of man's 'falsifying dream', no vision of the world. It is pure function: food is for consumption not thought:

> I sit in the top of the wood, my eyes closed.
> Inaction, no falsifying dream
> Between my hooked head and hooked feet:
> Or in sleep rehearse perfect kills and eat.

The hawk is a complete solipsist. The world is the world it sees and the creatures on it exist to assist the survival of the hawk. It believes itself to be God's supreme creation and is itself a Godlike arbiter of life and death:

> My feet are locked upon the rough bark.
> It took the whole of Creation
> To produce my foot, my each feather:
> Now I hold Creation in my foot.

Hughes has achieved a remarkable feat of empathy. But the poem is in his negative misanthropic vein. For the point of 'Hawk Roosting' is not so much to praise the hawk as to denigrate man. With its purely functional purpose built into its blood and feathers the hawk is seen as vastly superior to man who is unable to accept nature for what it is, and instead attempts to tame it by calling it philosophical names. The hawk has none of man's debilitating intellectuality, nor his slavish adherence to rules:

> There is no sophistry in my body:
> My manners are tearing off heads.

The same antithesis between functional animal and reflective man is made in 'Thrushes'. The birds eat to live and live to eat:

Terrifying are the attent sleek thrushes on the lawn,
More coiled steel than living—a poised
Dark deadly eye, those delicate legs
Triggered to stirrings beyond sense—with a start, a
    bounce, a stab
Overtake the instant and drag out some writhing thing.
No indolent procrastinations and no yawning stares,
No sighs or head-scratchings. Nothing but bounce and
    stab
And a ravening second.

To Hughes this murderously pure function, 'this bullet and automatic/Purpose' puts the thrushes on a level with 'Mozart's brain' and 'the shark's mouth'. By comparison man comes off badly—Mozart, of course, was no mere man so is exempt—and is reduced to physically sterile life in his ivory tower 'Carving at a tiny ivory ornament/For years'.

In 'February' Hughes laments the passing of the wolves. All that remains of them are pale shadows in tales for children in which man unfairly triumphs: 'The wolf with its belly stitched full of big pebbles . . . or that long grin/Above the naked coverlet'. In civilised Britain the wolf has been reduced to 'mere Alsatian'. Fixing on 'A photograph: the hairless, knuckled feet/Of the last wolf killed in Britain'—and conveniently forgetting the facts of the terrifying injuries inflicted by 'mere Alsatians' on town children—Hughes advocates a 'search/For their vanished head, for the world/Vanished with the head, the teeth, the quick eyes'. This poem manifests a longing for the good old bad old days when a man was a man and a wolf was a wolf and primitivism rubbed man's face in the earth. For in accordance with his matrist outlook on the world—a love of mother-earth and a near-Oedipal resentment against father-heaven—Hughes constantly strips man of his pretensions and places his feet firmly on the ground.

When Hughes uses animals to denigrate man the result is negative and counter-productive, for he is incapable of convincing the reader that man is an evolutionary aberration. For, artists aside, man is not a weak-kneed, pathetic, spiritually inclined creature of indolent procrastination. He is more vicious and destructive than any instinctive animal. At times Hughes sees the animal in a truly human perspective and it is then that his dissatisfaction with man is at its most convincing. 'An Otter' involves an animal who is the loser, a victim of man's gratuitous violence. For me, 'An Otter' is the finest poem Hughes has written so far. It reveals Hughes as a wonderfully gifted observer and also as a man who can make weighty conclusions on human behaviour. It demonstrates a magnificent poetic ability to conjure up out of the thin air of words the panache and movement of an animal.

'An Otter' begins with a burst of mimetic rhythm that sets the amphibian otter gliding through the water:

> Underwater eyes, an eel's
> Oil of water body, neither fish nor beast is the otter:
> Four-legged yet water-gifted, to outfish fish;
> With webbed feet and long ruddering tail
> And a round head like an old tomcat.

Hughes is clearly delighted by the ease with which the otter moves in two elements, air and water. He combines naturalistic information ('Does not take root like the badger') with an extraordinary insight into the motivation of the otter who is seen as a searcher, an animal 'Seeking/Some world lost when first he dived'. It is not the charm of the creature that Hughes celebrates, but its genetically inbuilt store of endless energy, its ingenuity of movement. The unrhymed five-line stanzas ripple with verbal understanding of this movement ('outfish fish', 'Wanders, cries', 'cleaves the stream's push till he licks', 'Walloping up roads with the milk wagon'), the lines themselves overlap like uneven waves in a river. The otter's effortless activity is infectious.

In the second half of the poem the rhythm changes abruptly. From a liquid accumulation of vowels ('eyes', 'eel's/Oil', 'outfish', 'Gallops along', 'melting', 'holes of lakes', 'licks/The pebbles', 'old shape', 'Walloping') the verbal texture is absorbed in the march of quatrains. Man has entered the otter's element and brings his 'tobacco-smoke, hounds and parsley'. It is the otter-hunting season and man, with his monotonously regular sense of occasion, moves in for the kill, arrives to put an end to the otter's energy as if its movement challenged his own slow tread. Nor does man come to kill the otter for any functional reason. He comes to conquer him so he can transform the otter into a trophy for his mate. The otter

> Yanked above hounds, reverts to nothing at all,
> To this long pelt over the back of a chair.

The otter kills—Hughes has 'no falsifying dream' about the nature of animals—but for a purpose. His killings are crimes of function. Man's murder of the otter's energy is a gratuitous act of violence. He destroys nature to reduce it to ornamentation.

At his best Hughes has no contemporary able to equal his advocacy of the cause of animals. He is uniquely able to bring them to life on the page. He makes no apology for them but offers a verbal incantation of their energetic essence. 'A Dream of Horses' has triplets rhyming *a b a* so Hughes can pound home the presence of the animals: the middle line of each stanza ends on 'horses' and in the last stanza the three line-endings are 'horses', 'horses' and 'horses'. Primitive man drew animals (like Hughes's mammoths) on cave walls to capture their spirit: Hughes is enough of a primitive to follow this precedent. In the twenty-seven lines of the poem horses are mentioned fourteen times. The whole method of writing is deliberately repetitive, the words are struck like hammer-blows: 'There shook hooves and hooves and hooves of horses'. The narrator is a groom who, speaking for his fellows, tells how, in a dream, 'we longed for a death trampled by such horses', and how, in waking, there remains the wish: 'Now let us, tied, be quartered by these poor horses'. The groom is so overwhelmed by the horses that he wishes only to submit to their superior energy, to die happy in their physical force. Hughes likes his animals to have a life of their own, as the horses do.

'View of a Pig' is a lament for a dead animal that man has reduced to 'Just so much/A poundage of lard and pork'. He has deprived the pig of the dignity of death as well as the 'earthly pleasure' of life. In an attempt to dignify the death of the pig Hughes resurrects the animal in his memory before the reader's eyes. He restores it to life:

Once I ran at a fair in the noise
To catch a greased piglet
That was faster and nimbler than a cat,
Its squeal was the rending of metal.

Pigs must have hot blood, they feel like ovens.
Their bite is worse than a horse's—
They chop a half-moon clean out.
They eat cinders, dead cats.

Yet all man sees in this bundle of animal energy is a carcass for the table. He takes it, kills it, packages it, then eats it in the lifeless luxury of his domestic cage. The slow heavy monosyllables of the poem—'It weighed, they said, as much as three men', 'It was like a sack of wheat'—and the scissory cutting edge of the key words ('pink, 'thick pink bulk', 'sack', 'Walking', 'factual', 'shocking', 'pathetic', 'squeal', 'scour') convey both the gravity of death and the sliced, plastic-packaged, fragmentary grave that awaits the pig.

As 'View of a Pig' shows, Hughes likes sharp, brittle, clicking, cutting words when he is writing about wounds. Such words onomatopoeically reproduce the sound of soft flesh being penetrated by sharp instruments. And instruments do not come any sharper than the big inward looking teeth of the pike. The pike is the most vicious, the most voracious of British freshwater fish. It devours other fish and has no qualms about eating other pike. Hughes verbally reproduces its fearsome bite with the snapping finality of his words: 'Pike', 'perfect Pike', 'killers', 'hooked clamp', 'pectorals', 'a vice locks', 'its film shrank', 'muscular tench'. This gives a harsh appropriate texture to the poem. In 'Pike' a pond is transformed into depth profound with hidden meanings:

A pond I fished, fifty yards across,
Whose lilies and muscular tench
Had outlasted every visible stone
Of the monastery that planted them—

> Stilled legendary depth:
> It was as deep as England. It held
> Pike too immense to stir, so immense and old
> That past nightfall I dared not cast.

Hughes is able to see a prehistoric past in the animal present and relishes the pike-eat-pike world of the lake, so different from the safety-first ambiance of civilised man. The pike, with its sharp teeth, its 'malevolent aged grin', is a completely functional creature: 'A life subdued to its instrument'. This, of course, is territory familiar to readers of Hughes's poetry and if each animal poem did no more than reiterate that point then Hughes would lose his readers as quickly as he captures animal illustrations of it. But the philosophical skeleton of the poems is not what matters. It is the vivid flesh that Hughes reproduces in words that refer to physical reality, not to abstract concepts. He tells of having three pike, then there were two, then one. Even the dead ones he retrieves in a lust of possession:

> Two, six pounds each, over two feet long,
> High and dry and dead in the willow-herb—
>
> One jammed past its gills down the other's gullet:
> The outside eye stared: as a vice locks—
> The same iron in this eye
> Though its film shrank in death.

The poem 'Bullfrog' is not as weighty as 'View of a Pig' or 'Pike', nowhere near as solid. It is a pencil-sketch whereas the other two are full-scale compositions that stretch the reader's whole mind. In 'The Bull Moses' Hughes's expectations are fulfilled. Precisely because the bull bulked larger than a boy's life and was supremely indifferent to his childish concerns;

> He would swing his muzzle at a fly
> But the square of sky where I hung, shouting, waving,
> Was nothing to him; nothing of our light
> Found any reflection in him.

What Hughes admires about the bull is his inhuman lack of concern for the life around him. And, as we would expect, the human beings that Hughes most admires are those who live most like animals. In 'The Bull Moses' the animal is admired for

> the warm weight of his breathing,
> The ammoniac reek of his litter, the hotly-tongued
> Mash of his cud . . .
> The brow like masonry, the deep-keeled neck

while the local Heptonstall worthy in 'Dick Straightup' is bull-like in his simplicity:

> His belly strong as a tree bole . . .
> > His upright walk,
> His strong back. . . .

Dick is a bull of a man who achieves legendary status as a colossus of the boozing fraternity: 'he emptied/Every Saturday the twelve-pint tankard at a tilt'. Even in old age his legend endures, for

> The young men sitting
> Taste their beer as by imitation,
> Borrow their words as by impertinence
> Because he sits there so full of legend and life
> Quiet as a man alone.

Like the bull Moses he is self-contained, indifferent to the petty life around. It is all very well for Hughes to pay posthumous tribute to such a man, 'strong as the earth you have entered', but there is also something deeply reactionary in this insistence that the present generation is so vastly inferior to the generation of real men who survived the so-called Great War which so fascinates Hughes. Just as he pokes fun at man in general by comparing his 'indolent procrastination' to the instinctive energy of animals, so he ridicules the present generation by making them pale pathetic shadows of their mighty elders. In our time 'thin clerks exercise/In their bed-sitters at midnight', poor pathetic creatures, whereas the mighty boozer Dick Straightup acted like an animal, getting roaring drunk, falling in the gutter, and surviving it: 'He was chipped out at dawn/Warm as a pie and snoring'.

There is an identical reactionary note in 'The Retired Colonel'. He, too, is like a bull: 'Brow bull-down for the stroke'. He, too, is a great drinker: 'Shot through the heart with whisky'. He, too, possesses 'ancient courage'. Or so Hughes tells us. Worse, he rhetorically asks:

> And what if his sort should vanish?
> The rabble starlings roar upon
> Trafalgar. The man-eating British lion
> By a pimply age brought down.

Hughes then compares the blimp to that other creature dear to his heart: 'the last English wolf' (the same wolf that appeared in 'February'). A third reactionary poem, 'Fourth of July', sneers at American Independence Day. Hughes links the discovery of America by Columbus with the passing of brute animal force, 'Killing the last of the mammoths'. And far from being independent —like a bull, like Dick Straightup, like the Retired Colonel— man is adrift in his own aimlessness:

> Now the mind's wandering elementals . . .
> Wait dully at the traffic crossing,
> Or lean over headlines, taking nothing in.

As a comment on life it is even more confused than Yeats's anti-democratic hymns to power. For Hughes would substitute for our 'pimply age'—if *he* paid more attention to the headlines he would find our age far from 'pimply'—an icebound battleground on which Dick Straightup would no doubt outdrink the pike, and the Retired Colonel would do battle with the mammoths. Hughes is more successful as an informed observer than as a weighty thinker.

The comparison with Yeats is not merely political for there are five poems in *Lupercal* on Yeatsian witches and tramps. 'Things Present' tells of the dream of 'A bare-backed tramp' in a ditch. He has nothing but his dream, which is about his ancestors. In fact they were crofters living under a thatched roof, 'A roof treed to deflect death'. In the tramp's fantasy 'My sires had towers and great names'. This dream is clearly not enough to ward off the fury of the elements for the tramp reappears in 'The Good Life' as a hermit who has returned to the world. He has learned that physical poverty leads to spiritual poverty not Zarathustrian wisdom. Bitter experience of poverty has taught him that 'Only a plump, cuffed citizen/Gets enough quiet to hear God speak'. So on his return to the world he is determined to be humble enough to receive the charity, if not the respect, of the wealthy:

> Loud he prayed then; but late or early
> Never a murmur came to his need
> Save 'I'd be delighted!' and 'Yours sincerely',
> And 'Thank you very much indeed!'

'Witches' invokes the black-magical past when 'Once was every woman the witch' in order to pour some more scorn on our 'pimply age'. Hughes believes, or wants to believe, in a mysterious past when miracles were everyday occurrences and lusty witches satisfied lucky men. In this obscurantist mood he also wants to believe that our age's scientific scepticism is merely a safety-first strait-jacket thrown on the dark forces we ignore at our peril. His rhetorical question refuses to believe that witchcraft was mere superstition:

> Did they dream it?
> Oh, our science says they did.
> It was all wishfully dreamed in bed.
> Small psychology would unseam it.

Hughes pretends to know better.

The Yeatsian influence hangs over 'Singers'—with its 'curse on the age that loses the tune', a 'pimply age' of course—and 'Crag Jack's Apostasy'. Crag Jack is down on his luck, he has 'kicked at the world and slept in ditches'. Unlike the hermit in 'The Good Life', Crag Jack does 'not desire to change my ways'. All he wants is a bit of evidence of God's concern for him so he can 'Keep more than the memory/Of a wolf's head, of eagles' feet'. In 'November' the Yeatsian elements are put into a place of Hughes's own making, the dark world of the elements. There is a ditch, and, inevitably, a tramp in it. He is asleep, apparently dead, but actually alive with the life of nature herself:

> his stillness separated from the death
> Of the rotting grass and the ground. A wind chilled,
> And a fresh comfort tightened through him,
> Each hand stuffed deeper into the other sleeve.

What Hughes admires in this tramp in his ability to coexist with the elements:

> I stayed on under the welding cold
>
> Watching the tramp's face glisten and the drops on his
>   coat
> Flash and darken. I thought what strong trust
> Slept in him—as the trickling furrows slept,
> And the thorn-roots in their grip on darkness.

This image of man at one with his elements, away from the omnirestrictive domestic cage, leads Hughes to a somewhat tendentious inconclusion. For he runs from the tramp smack into a gamekeeper's gibbet:

> The keeper's gibbet had owls and hawks
> By the neck, weasels, a gang of cats, crows.

Though they are dead 'Some still had their shape,/Had their pride with it'. 'Pride' seems entirely inappropriate to a dead animal deprived of its function.

This portrait of a figure in a landscape convinces me that Hughes is not at home with human beings—unless they are romantic caricatures like Dick Straightup and The Retired Colonel—in the way he is with animals in a landscape at the mercy of the elements. 'A Woman Unconscious' is a noble attempt to isolate one death to emphasise the enormity of imminent global immolation by nuclear bomb. For as 'Russia and America circle each other' in posture of men at combat

> Did a lesser death come
>
> Onto the white hospital bed
> Where one, numb beyond her last of sense,
> Closed her eyes on the world's evidence
> And into pillows sunk her head.

That makes some amends for the absurdity of designating the present as merely a 'pimply age'.

The title poem is set in Rome. Lupercalia was a perverse Roman festival when goats and a dog were sacrificed and when sterile women were supposedly made fertile after priests had whipped them with goatskin thongs. Typically, Hughes finds the most distasteful aspect of this orgy of irrationality the sacrifice of the animals, because 'The dog loved its churlish life' while the goats possess 'Spirit of the ivy,/Stink of goat, of a rank thriving'. As for the unfortunate women, they, in their sterility, are the living dead:

> This woman's as from death's touch: a surviving
> Barrenness: she abides; perfect,
> But flung from the wheel of the living,
> The past killed in her, the future plucked out.

Hughes empathises rather with the priests beating the women, their action perfectly symbolising ritualistic irrationality:

> Fresh thongs of goat-skin
> In their hands they go bounding past,
> And deliberate welts have snatched her in
>
> To the figure of racers. Maker of the world,
> Hurrying the lit ghost of man
> Age to age while the body hold,
> Touch this frozen one.

When Hughes admits himself to his poetry he is exempt from the criticisms the poems thrash into man. He is a man alone with the elements, most at home in the Pennines, 'these dark hills' as he calls them in 'Fire-Eater'. It is, therefore, natural that some of his best poems are landscapes. 'Mayday on Holderness' (Holderness is a peninsula in the East Riding of Yorkshire overlooking Hull on the Humber) contains this self-portrait of Hughes in a landscape:

> Birth-soils,
> The sea-salts, scoured me, cortex and intestine,
> To receive these remains.
> As the incinerator, as the sun,
> As the spider, I had a whole world in my hands.
> Flowerlike, I loved nothing.

As he watches the river Humber snaking away he feels, inside him, a serpent—a visceral disturbance—that makes a return to childhood innocence impossible for Hughes:

> What a length of gut is growing and breathing—
> This mute eater, biting though the mind's
> Nursery floor, with eel and hyena and vulture,
> With creepy-crawly and the root,
> With the sea-worm entering its birthright.

The serpent inside him is the biblical serpent that destroys Eden-like innocence. Although 'Couples at their pursuits are laughing in the lanes' Hughes cannot submit to innocent pastimes. He has in him the knowledge of evil, the serpent, and a childhood filled with Bill Hughes's stories of 'the pierced helmet./Cordite oozings of Gallipoli'. So Hughes has war in his brain and a serpent in his belly. Knowledge of nightmares and irrepressible myth-memories of serpents:

> Cordite oozings of Gallipoli,
> Curded to beastings, broached my palate,
> The expressionless gaze of the leopard,

The coils of the sleeping anaconda,
The nightlong frenzy of shrews.

What solace he can find is in his intimate relationship with the hills of his childhood, the east Yorkshire Pennines. In 'Pennines n April' these rainsodden hills are compared to massive waves, they move in Hughes's imagination:

Landscapes gliding blue as water
Those barrellings of strength are heaving slowly and
      heave
To your feet and surf upwards
In a still, fiery air, hauling the imagination,
Carrying the larks upward.

When Hughes's imagination is not being hauled upwards by the Pennines it is delving deep into water. In 'Pike' he saw legendary depths, in 'To Paint a Water Lily' (a title that derives from Monet's great impressionist evocations of water lilies) he sees

Prehistoric bedragonned times
Crawl that darkness with Latin names.

This poem, written in couplets, is a companion piece to 'October Dawn' from *The Hawk in the Rain*. In the earlier poem the poet imagined a new ice age. In 'To Paint a Water Lily' he has no need to imagine more than what lurks beneath the surface. For the creatures of the pond 'Have evolved no improvements there,/ Jaws for heads, the set stare,/Ignorant of age as of hour'. They are stuck in a timeless world of unadulterated function and are uncontaminated by intellect.

In 'Mayday on Holderness' Hughes described himself as 'Flowerlike'. With his intimate knowledge of nature he does not associate flowers with a purely decorative submissive beauty. No, the flower has to struggle to survive as much as the animal does. In 'Snowdrop' he reverses the traditional connotations of the flower. Far from merely existing, the snowdrop has to struggle against the earth, has to push and assert itself in order to survive:

> She, too, pursues her ends,
> Brutal as the stars of this month,
> Her pale head heavy as metal.

The overall impression of *Lupercal* is that Hughes has a vision both God-like and obsessively earth-bound. It is as if he were able to see things from the perspective of deep space, see the globe as if it were the light at the end of a massive tunnel. At times Hughes seems to think that if he blinked the globe would disappear, so he stares even harder and takes the occasional microscopic view of a detail, as in 'Snowdrop'. The danger in such a vision is that the tunnel will become more significant than the light—the world—at the end of it.

Lupercal was published in March 1960. The following month Frieda Rebecca, the first child of Ted Hughes and Sylvia Plath, was born. It is not so surprising then that Hughes's next book was addressed to children. *Meet My Folks!*, which appeared in April 1961, made great fun of an imaginary Hughes family. For example the poem 'My Brother Bert' takes as its starting point the fact that Ted's real brother Gerald used to keep animals. In the poem this hobby assumes gigantic proportions:

> The very thought makes me iller and iller:
> Bert's brought home a gigantic Gorilla!
>
> If you think that's really not such a scare,
> What if it quarrels with his Grizzly Bear?

And so on.

On 17 January 1962 a son, Nicholas Ferrar, was born to Ted Hughes and Sylvia Plath. On 11 February 1963 Sylvia Plath took her life. Hughes was thus left with two children and his concern for them is reflected in the publications that followed *Meet my Folks!* Hughes chose to concentrate on books for children and it was not until May 1967 that he aimed another general book at an adult audience. In November 1963, ten months after the death of Sylvia Plath, he published two books for children, in prose and verse respectively: *How the Whale Became* and *The*

Earth-Owl and other Moon-People. The last book was not calculated to reassure children for it imagined a moon populated by creatures out of nightmares. Take 'The Adaptable Mountain Dugong' escaping from death:

> For instance, here comes a pack of wild dogs, each with
>   a mouth like a refuse bin.
> They have smelt the Mountain Dugong's peculiar
>   fried fish smell and want to get their teeth in,
> Because wild dogs need to devour every living thing in
>   all directions and to them this is no sin.
>
> But the Mountain Dugong is already prepared, the
>   wild dogs cannot shock it.
> He unscrews his table-legs and screws a greyhound leg
>   into each socket.
> And is off over the crater-edge with all his equipment in
>   three leaps like a rubber rocket.

Hughes continued his pedogogic role thereafter as if absorption in the world of children would offer him some relief from the darkly sinister forces he felt gripped the adult world. He published a book of narrative doggerel for children, *Nessie the Mannerless Monster*, in April 1964. He helped judge the *Daily Mirror* Children's Literary Competition. He prepared a series of broadcasts for the BBC Schools Broadcasting Department (later published as *Poetry in the Making* in the UK, and *Poetry Is* in the USA). However, Hughes had not relinquished his most serious concern: the poetry that lurked inside him like a serpent. When it came out it seemed as if the universe of Ted Hughes's imagination was a darker place than ever. It was not a question of there being no God, but of there being a God capable of monstrous blunders and black sense of humour, whose sickest joke was the creation of man.

4 'Man Turning Angel'

When Thom Gunn was bidding farewell to his 'sad captains' in San Francisco, he was clearly ready for an important change of direction, of poetic motivation. He had put a lot of himself into his poetry and he seemed to want to experience the world for what it is, rather than for what it became inside his ego. In 1964 Gunn came to London for a year to work on a book with his brother, the photographer Ander. After ten years in the USA Thom Gunn was ready to have a close look at life as she is lived in London. As far as possible this would include the whole gamut of London life: the rich and the poor, the young and the old, the manual workers and the out-of-work, the newly born and old folk tottering on the edge of death. The book, comprising thirty-seven poems and thirty-nine photographs (one of which is an enlarged detail of a previous photograph) appeared in November 1966—the same year that Gunn decided to give up his teaching job at Berkeley.

Sensitivity to visual images was nothing new in Gunn's work. One of his finest poems, 'In Santa Maria del Popolo' from *My Sad Captains,* worked verbal conclusions out of Caravaggio's visual composition. Yet that is a different matter entirely from publishing poems opposite photographs. 'In Santa Maria del Popolo' does not completely depend on Caravaggio's painting, just as Auden's 'Musée des Beaux Arts' does not completely depend on Breughel's 'The Fall of Icarus'. We do not need to have the picture reproduced beside such poems in order to understand them. In *Positives* the side-by-side layout of the book was a sure sign that the poem needed the picture as much as the picture needed the poem. The two were meant to represent an artistic coexistence.

Clearly the title of the book is not simply a reference to positive photographic prints but an indication of Gunn's attitude to his subject-matter. In alliance with his brother's visual images Gunn goes out to give vivid impressions of real people in real situations. There are no symbolic figures or embodiments of philosophy. It is a poetry of selective observation, not a poetry of cogitation. And the relaxation of content brings a relaxation of style. There is more conversational flow. Several of the poems are, in fact, supposed to be people talking, and they talk authentically. In poems like 'Lofty in the Palais de Danse' *(Fighting Terms)* and 'The Unsettled Motorcyclist's Vision of his Death' *(The Sense of Movement)* we had to suspend our disbelief about tearaways talking in metre and rhyme. In *Positives* he verbally snaps the speech so that a little girl says

> In a bus it is nice to ride on top because
> it looks like running people over

while a barmaid likes her pub because it is cosy

> not like them redecorated
> pubs down Chelsea.

Positives is Gunn's first book in free verse, and the sort of free verse he favours is that associated with William Carlos Williams: simple and conversational and rooted in the objects that are being described. The only use of rhyme in the whole book is for humorous effect when he writes a mock-hymn to that British institution, tea-drinking:

> *When God bade labour for our burden, He*
> *Relented slightly at the end,*
> *And granted respite twice a day, for tea.*
> *O Teapot, heavenly maid, descend.*

I do not want to make over large claims for *Positives*. Gunn, for example, once referred to it with the offhand remark: 'my brother Ander did the photographs and I did verse captions to them'.[1] Yet I think it was an important bridge for Gunn to cross. The fact that the poems had to interrelate with the photographs

---

1 Autobiographical note written for Faber & Faber, November 1972.

meant that Gunn had to pin his thought down on the surface of reality. There was simply no justification for Metaphysical self-indulgent free-association. There was no place in the book for striking heroic poses. For once we could *see* the people he was writing about. They existed, they were not introduced to make philosophical points.

The theme of *Positives* is change and transformation: through aging, through civic demolition, through social status. There is no naive view that everyone has a limitless number of choices dancing in front of him waiting to be picked, rather a realisation that social factors play an enormous part in the development of the human species. Everyone may be born with a beautiful potential but not everyone gets the opportunity to fulfil that potential. So the book opens with an unaccompanied photograph of a newly born baby. This is, as it were, the raw material that will either impose action and insights on the world or, on the other hand, be condemned by social pressure to submit to the vagaries of economic underprivilege. With this photograph it has still all to happen. The child could end up as anything for we are given no information about it. It could be a baby born in Buckingham Palace or a baby born in the Glasgow Gorbals.

In stark contrast is the old lady who closes *Positives*. The book began with the promise of birth. It ends with the recognition of death. The old lady first appears in 'The mould from baked beans that'. She sleeps near an abandoned home. She sleeps on old papers. In 'Poking around the rubbish' the old lady remembers her past:

> Near Maidstone once, hop-picking
> with the four babies and Tom,
> she worked all day along the green
> alleys, among the bins
> in the dim leafy light of
> the overhanging vines.

But her memory is failing and she has only a vague impression of what happened: 'Tom took something! What was it?' She is old and decrepit and is losing even her momory. The book ends with a tribute to the old lady's attitude to death. The poem

'Something approaches, about' (entitled 'The Old Woman' in *Poems 1950–1966: A Selection*) describes the old woman's awareness of death, while the accompanying photograph depicts her terror. Her life is so utterly without meaning that death cannot be any worse:

> Let it come, it is
> the terror of full repose,
> and so no terror.

Positives is a superb minor achievement, a plain-speaking meditation on the wastage of so much human life. The old lady in the final poem is like the old women in 'In Santa Maria del Popolo' *(My Sad Captains)*. When he approaches a theme like this Gunn shows a genuine compassion and this is the essential quality that will ensure the growth of his talent. No amount of technical virtuosity could compensate for the arrogant cynicism with which he cloaked his sensitivity in *Fighting Terms* and *The Sense of Movement*. *Positives* is important from the technical point of view in that it demonstrated Gunn's ability to dispense with his metrical strait jacket (essential wear with the cynical cloak of the first two books). Here he uses free verse in the style of William Carlos Williams and he uses it well.

As we have seen, Gunn dropped out of Berkeley in 1966, the year of *Positives*. The following year he published *Touch* in which a further stage in the growth of this compassion was revealed. This is his description of the book.

> I think *Touch* shows a kind of development in attitudes
> from those of my earlier books. The point of the title
> must be obvious, as it is directly relevant to most of the
> poems in the book: the touch is not physical only, it is
> meant to be an allegory for the touch of sympathy that
> should be the aim of human intercourse. . . . I do not
> mean that one can simply love everybody because one
> wants to, but that one can try to avoid all the situations
> in which love is impossible [2]

2 *Poetry Book Society Bulletin No 54*, London, September 1967.

In one way the book differs from the previous volumes in that it contains two extended sequences: 'Confessions of the Life Artist' and 'Misanthropos'. The danger of being a creative artist is the possibility of a descent into the belief that other people are merely there to provide ideas and inspirations for works of art. Gunn's Life Artist, who narrates the poem in the first person (and who speaks throughout the ten sections of the poem in unrhymed lines of seven syllables) has just such an attitude:

> Whatever is here, it is
> material for my art.

He believes himself to be God-like because of his ability

> Circling over a city,
> to reject the thousand, and
> to select the one.

In seeing people as potential artistic prototypes he must, however, lose his respect for their humanity, which in turn makes him a little less than human.

A more philosophical view of mankind permeates 'Misanthropos' which must stand as Gunn's supreme narrative achievement to date. It is by far the longest poem he has published and it develops a unique tone from the tension between Gunn's two ways of approaching the world: the path of reason and the path of instinct. Both ways are thoroughly explored in 'Misanthropos'. The poem is in four parts: 'The Last Man' comprising five sections; 'Memoirs of the World' in six sections; 'Elegy on the Dust' which is a single poem; and the five-section finale 'The First Man'.

Poem 1 of 'Misanthropos' (first person narration, rhyming triplets of nine-syllable lines) presents the basic situation from which the internal drama of the whole sequence derives. Believing himself to be the only man left in the world ('the final man walks the final hill'), Man decides that his chances of survival will be greater if he surrenders to instinct and eliminates his consciousness. So 'He lives like/the birds, self-contained'. The headwound of anguish means that

> a relentless
> memory of monstrous battle is
> keener than counsel of the senses.

So, choosing his salvation, Man 'opens, then, a disused channel/ to the onset of hatred'.

Poem II (first person narration in broken couplets of iambic pentameter and modelled on a device similar to that in Sir Philip Sidney's poem 'Echo') states the enormity of Man's predicament. He shouts desperately in a canyon, hoping to hear another voice. But what he hears is his own echo distorted by his growing reliance on instinct:

> What have I left, who stood among mankind,
> When the firm base is undermined?
>
> A mind.
>
> Yet, with a vacant landscape as its mirror,
> What can it choose, to ease the terror?
>
> Error.
>
> Is there no feeling, then, that I can trust,
> In spite of what we have discussed?
>
> Disgust.

So, as a result of this dialogue with himself, he puts his trust in disgust. Poem III (third person narration, blank verse) has Gunn relating the predicament of Man to his consistent search for identity. As a soldier the Man had no problem knowing who he was. But surviving the holocaust he found 'His uniform was peeling from his back'. He has thus lost one identity and must fashion another out of his extremity. He must become an animal, a creature of instinct, so he makes himself a dress from animal skin: 'His poverty is a sort of uniform'. Though alone he is still a Man, 'A courier after identity'.

Poem IV (third person narration, terza-rima) is a hymn of hatred to consciousness—'the flaw' Man has to bear. It is night and Man sees the Milky Way, his geocentric view of the centre of his galaxy. The moon is a 'dead globe' unlike the earth. Man envies it for being so. For, in his way of looking at it, the creation of the earth was followed by 'two more births...Life, consciousness, like linked catastrophes'. Animals were fortunate in avoiding the second of these catastrophes, consciousness, which carries with it a painful ability to differentiate oneself from the universe instead of accepting it. It also carries the burden of the past, 'the inheritance he did not choose,/As he accepted drafting for that war'. Still watching the moon, Man thinks of the 'clearest light in the whole universe': the sun. Poem V (third person, seven-syllable lines rhyming *a b c a b c*) presents a geography of the earth which shows it in lush contrast to the sterile moon of the previous poem. Among this vegetation, without which life could not exist, Man remakes himself in an animal image: 'Nothing moves/at the edges of the mind'. This ends the first part of 'Misanthropos'.

The second part of the poem, 'Memoirs of the World' (entirely in first-person narration giving Man's recollection of himself) comprises six sections. Poem VI (basically iambic pentameter rhyming *a b a b c d c d* with a mimetic bird-call refrain of 'Not now, not now, not now') shows him at the mercy of his memory. For watching a setting sun he cannot perceive it as an isolated phenomenon. It 'calls old sunsets to my mind' when his plea is 'Let me live, one second'. The workings of his memory place him in the past when he feels it necessary to live in the present:

> Most poignant and most weakening, that recall.
> Although I lived from day to day, too, there.

Poem VII (seven-syllable lines rhyming *a b c a b c*) is a self-portrait of Man as a poseur. He wore dark glasses, he 'stood/an armed angel among men'. He was never able to transcend this pose, he was subject to 'an indecision,/a hunger in the senses' and passed his time in pointless fidgeting or fingering 'some doorjamb'. As a poseur 'I was presence without full/being'.

In this mood of self-pity we turn to the present in Poem VIII (*a b a b* quatrains of iambic pentameter). He has made a fire in which he becomes absorbed, trying to see shapes in it, 'studying to remember/What the world was, and meant'. His imaginative free-association conjures up Dryads, tree-spirits, whose insubstantial presence urges him to ponder on the essence of evil. Does it exist as a force of nature or is there simply 'pain, evil's external mark'? In this mood he longs for human company, someone more worthy than himself, 'A man who burnt from sympathy alone'. For the Man in 'Misanthropos' has been no hero, but 'A serving man' as Poem IX ('unrhymed stanzas of six seven-syllable lines) informs us.

Poem X (couplets of nine-syllable lines) offers a nightmare vision of the origin of human life. Man is blinded by staring aimlessly at the vast stretches of snow before him. He seems to be looking at 'the emptiness./A negative of matter'. This would appear to be the physical equivalent of the elimination of conciousness he has been trying to achieve. But the encroaching blank emptiness frightens him and 'my mind loses hold'. At the mercy of his nightmare he sees the beginnings of life on earth. First there are unicellular creatures 'swimming in concert/like nebulae, calm, without effort'. Into this peace the first human cell blunders like an invasion. This cell can only reproduce by coupling with other cells:

> it touches it holds, in an act of
> enfolding, possessing, merging love.
>
> There is coupling where no such should be
> Surely it is a devil, surely
>
> It is life's parody I see, which
> enthralls a universe with its rich
>
> heavy passion, leaving behind it
> gorgeous mutations only, then night.

In this physical, biological necessity to possess other people Man sees the great predicament of mankind: human beings are not self-contained. He decides to short-circuit the electrical force of his imaginative reason:

> I must keep to the world's bare surface,
> I must perceive, and perceive what is.

Yet there is one final memory of a good man. Poem XI, 'Epitaph for Anton Schmidt' (eight- and nine-syllable lines rhyming *a b c b*), is a tribute to a man who acted unselfishly out of a disinterested love of humanity. For such an action he was executed. But his action partly redeems an otherwise despicable species:

> He never did mistake for bondage
> The military job, the chances,
> The limits; he did not submit
> To the blackmail of his circumstances.
>
> I see him in the Polish snow,
> His muddy wrappings small protection,
> Breathing the cold air of his freedom
> And treading a distinct direction.

The third part of 'Misanthropos' consists of one poem, Poem XII, 'Elegy on the Dust' (third person narration, couplets of alternating pentameters and tetrameters). In the absence of humanity there is no possibility of a disinterested action like that performed by Anton Schmidt. Human beings do indeed need other human beings. Now

> the human race, too, lies
> An imperfection endlessly refined
> By the imperfection of the mind.

This encapsulates in elegant verse the concept that tool-making man's greatness lies in what he's not. Lacking physical equipment for survival, mankind constructed houses, cities and—finally—weapons of destruction, his supremely human creation. Mankind has contrived its own extinction.

The finale of 'Misanthropos' comprises five poems collectively entitled 'The First Man'. Several years have passed since 'Elegy on the Dust'. Man has now regressed to a primitive anthropoid type, almost neolithic in appearance. Man has achieved his ambition: he has substituted animal instinct for human consciousness. Poem XIII (third person narration, four-stress lines modelled on Eliot's diction in 'Four Quartets') presents the state of Man's regression:

Is he a man? If man is cogitation,
This is at most a rudimentary man,
An unreflecting organ of perception;
Slow as a bull, in moving; yet, in taking,
Quick as an adder. He does not dream at night.

He is now pure animal function: 'He is a nose./He picks through
the turned earth, and eats. A mouth.' (This metamorphosis into
preconceptual primitivism was one of the ambitions of the early
Gunn, though at that stage of his development he could not
have conceived what self-contained primitivism would mean.)

In Poem XIV (third person narration, syllabic count of
4.10.6.10.10. rhyming *a a b c b c*) consciousness is reborn. And
with the birth of consciousness comes the birth of its instrument,
the word. Man is startled because other men are approaching
and at their approach his uniquely human faculties—perception,
language, classification—reassert themselves:

> 'What is it? What?'
> Mouth struggles with the words that mind forgot.
>   While from the high brown swell
> He watches it, the smudge, he sees it grow
> As it crawls closer, crawls unturnable
> And unforeseen upon the plain below.

Alarmed and exhilarated, at once he thinks of washing in a
nearby pool so he will appear utterly different from those who
approach. But he hesitates because his body no longer wants to
be self-contained and separate. With this essentially human
concern he changes, he becomes 'a little more upright,/In picturing
man almost becomes man too'.

Poem XV (third person narration, couplets of iambic pentameter) describes the approach of the other survivors, 'forty
men and women'. As Man watches them from his hiding place
behind a rock he sees one man stumble and come close to the
hiding place. With his sharpened senses Man hears this human
gasp for air, sees the 'ribbed bony creature'. What finally moves
him to renew human contact is seeing some scratches on the
human's chest. At the sight of this wound

> He walks around to where the creature leans.
> The creature sees him, jumps back, staggers, calls,
> Then, losing balance on the pebbles, falls.

Still a human impulse is urging Man on, and so

> He stops, bewildered by his force, and then
> Lifts up the other to his feet again.

The narrative is taken up by Man himself in Poem XVI (unrhymed seven-syllable lines). He sees that the man he has helped is no heroic man of action. Nevertheless he is a human being and Man overcomes his misanthropic disgust to accept this human as a creature worthy of respect and trust. The final poem, Poem XVII (*a b a b* quatrains alternating iambic pentameter with syllabic lines), makes a general conclusion from this particular meeting. Men come from dust and return to dust. But this does not mean that they should denigrate either themselves or other men. The origin of the human species is not the point: the achievement of humanity is. And to survive *as a human being* each man has to trust and touch with feeling his fellow man:

> Turn out toward others, meeting their look at full,
>   Until you have completely stared
> On all there is to see. Immeasurable,
>   The dust yet to be shared.

'Misanthropos' is Gunn's most sustained achievement to date. He has written individual poems superior to any one section of 'Misanthropos' ('In Santa Maria del Popolo' from *My Sad Captains,* or 'Sunlight' from *Moly* are examples that come to mind). But 'Misanthropos' demonstrates structural and thematic and narrative gifts that Gunn might profitably use again instead of unambitiously confining himself to virtually the one-page poem.

Nothing else in *Touch* compares in scope to the brilliant achievement of 'Misanthropos'. However, that sequence sets such a high standard that this is no condemnation. In fact *Touch* contains some of Gunn's most genuinely enjoyable poems, poems that avoid tortuous ratiocination and filter felt experience through a fragile surface of words. There is the title poem itself which Gunn considers 'My first successful free verse poem of any importance'.[3] This celebrates the possibility of reciprocal love, something that was rejected in *Fighting Terms* and *The Sense of Movement* where only sex existed, sex as aggressive assault, as taking. In 'Touch' the poet slips into bed beside a sleeping lover who turns and holds him. This gesture is unheroic but basic to the continued existence of humanity. The poet feels he could just as well be his lover's mother or 'the nearest human being to/hold onto in a/dreamed pogrom'. Gunn now sees a universal significance in the human embrace, succumbing to a dream of a universe which 'seeps/from our touch in/continuous creation'.

Instinct seems important to Gunn now only if it involves the human impulse (like the spontaneous touch in Poem XV of 'Misanthropos'). So when he invokes his muse of energy and instinct in 'The Goddess' it is not as an aid to self-contained discipline. Instead he draws the attention of the Goddess Proserpina with her immense vigour (capable of bursting 'up/through potholes and narrow flues/seeking an outlet') to 'vulnerable, quivering' human beings—the kind of human beings who need an energetic instinct of survival if they are to oppose men like 'the dark hysteric conqueror' (Hitler) of 'Berlin in Ruins'.

This compassionate concern for the fate of other, less fortunate people informs the best moments of *Touch*. One of the finest moments is 'In the Tank' which probes into the mental torment of a condemned man. In his early poems the most terrible prison for Gunn was the cave of mental sterility, the most terrible sentence (in more ways than one) was his being 'Condemned to life' ('Legal Reform', *The Sense of Movement*). In *Touch* he shows an admirable ability to break out of this atmosphere of egocentric self-pity. He has become aware of the suffering of other people. The felon suffers from being totally deprived of the touch of humanity:

> The jail contained a tank, the tank contained
> A box, a mere suspension, at the centre,
> Where there was nothing left to understand,
> And where he must re-enter and re-enter.

3 Letter, 7 October 1972.

As if to emphasise the genuine predicament of the felon and the intellectually simulated anguish of the intellectual Gunn includes 'Breakfast' where a man's biggest challenge is what to eat in the morning. For him 'toast/and coffee served as markers'. This man could be T.S. Eliot, the deracinated intensely cerebral intellectual, who 'measured out [his] life with coffee spoons' (in his *persona* in 'The Love Song of J. Alfred Prufrock').

Touch closes with 'Back to Life'. The image that is sustained throughout this poem is the familiar one of human beings as leaves all growing from a single branch on the tree of life. At first it seems as if Gunn is about to indulge in self-pity:

> I am alone, like a patrolling keeper.
> And then I catch the smell of limes
> Coming and going faintly on the dark.

Existential solitude was obligatory in Gunn's early poetry. Now he seeks the touch of humanity in other human beings. Just as the leaves can be perceived both as a mass and as a collection of unique little entities, so can 'the other strollers' in the street be apprehended as an undifferentiated mass or as an intermingling of individuals:

> the light revealed us all
> Sustained in delicate difference
> Yet firmly growing from a single branch.

So Gunn feels a part of the human race, not apart from it. It is a major switch in attitude. Yet, just as sunlight is needed for the photosynthetic growth of leaves on branches,

> The branch we grow on
> Is not remembered easily in the dark

so that people are at their most solitary and vulnerable at night (a predicament which has been solved since time immemorial by the acquisition of a sleeping partner). The poem celebrates the force of life, 'the sap that runs through' the bough

As if each leaf were, so, better prepared
For falling sooner or later separate.

Where *Fighting Terms* and *The Sense of Movement* were mainly remarkable for the showy display of literary erudition and Elizabethan metrics, *My Sad Captains* and *Touch* show Gunn maturing into a poet with something worth saying to other people. The discipline so insisted on in the two early books restricted Gunn the man as if the iambic lines of the poetry were iron bars trapping him in a cerebral prison. *My Sad Captains* and *Touch* liberated Gunn the man from the pose of Gunn the swaggering intellectual tough.

Gunn's personality is the dominant factor in *Moly*, the book that followed *Touch*. It was published in March 1971 and it uses, as a metaphor for man's spiritual illumination, the star whose light sustains human life, the sun: 'My blood, it is like light' ('Rites of Passage'); 'the ground/Is sun-stained' ('The Sand Man'); 'the heat that sponsors heat, from the sky' ('Three'); 'a sunlit bank of pale unflowering weed' ('Words'); 'Down-ribbed with shine' ('From the Wave'); 'light is in the pupil' ('Tom-Dobbin'); 'the gardens fill/With sunlight' ('The Rooftop'); 'Upon a platform dappled by the sun' ('The Fair in the Woods'); 'the intense undazzling light' ('The Garden of the Gods'); 'In sunlight now, after the weeks it rained' ('Flooded Meadows'); 'the dust of summer' ('Grasses'); 'Merely reflecting sunlight' ('The Discovery of the Pacific'); 'The whole side of a world facing the sun' ('Sunlight'). The book is a search for the spiritual sunlight that enhances each individual. It is also an attempt to describe a world of sensation that lies beyond the restricted consciousness of everyday life.

However, the spirituality of *Moly* is chemically-induced, for on one level the book is a celebration of the insights made possible by hallucinatory drugs. In Homer's *Odyssey*, Odysseus is rescued from Circe's spellbinding ability to turn men into swine when Hermes gives him a magic herb: the moly. In Gunn's book Circe is the society that reduces man to the level of his physical needs, LSD the magic herb that nullifies the dead hand of society. Gunn says 'I still think much the same about LSD....To put it at its simplest: it opens up possibilities in a man's life—they were always there, but he didn't realise it. Of course the possibilities depend on the man'.[4] Great claims have been made for the religious possibilities of LSD by those who regard it as a sacrament, but Gunn is not a proselytiser. What Gunn seems to have experienced under the influence of LSD is a sense of human Oneness, a surge of love for his fellow man, a perception of the vast complexity of the phenomenal world. Epistemological orthodoxy applauds man's classifying faculty, his mental habit of putting exterior experience into ordered compartments. Gunn has always been suspicious of intellectual classification. He has longed for preverbal, preconceptual experiences. Whether he has succeeded in communicating these insights is the test on which *Moly* stands or falls.

What Gunn has retained from his existentialist days is a belief that it is never too late to choose. This is his description of the thematic content of *Moly*:

> We can all take on the features of pigs—or what humans interpret as those features—we all have in us the germs of the brutal, greedy, and dull. And we can all avoid becoming pigs, though to do so we must be wily and self-aware. Moly [LSD] can help us to know our own potential for change: even though we are in the power of Circe or of time, we do not have to become pigs, we do not have to be unmanned, we are as free to make and unmake ourselves as we were at the age of ten...there are certainly other ways of looking at my book. It could be seen as a debate between the passion for definition and the passion for flow, it could be seen as a history of San Francisco from 1965–9, or as a personal memoir of myself during those years. But I think of it as being about Odysseus' meeting with Hermes, his eating of that herb, and his reflections on metamorphosis in the remaining walk he has before he reaches the thick stone-built house.[5]

4 Letter, 17 March 1974.
5 *Poetry Book Society Bulletin No. 68*, London, Spring 1971.

The point Gunn makes about San Francisco is vital. He has always been a poet who responds to the trends of his time and he could hardly have avoided the love-thy-neighbour-through-LSD atmosphere of San Francisco in the 1960s.

In the arrangement of the poems *Moly* resembles a psychedelic pop music album. A general mood of spiritual aspiration floats through all the poems but there are many changes of tempi and mood: fast numbers follow slow numbers, short tracks make way for longer 'far-out' explorations. The book opens with 'Rites of Passage' whose first line tells us that 'Something is taking place'. Metamorphosis is under way:

> Something is taking place.
> Horns bud bright in my hair.
> My feet are turning hoof.
> And Father, see my face
> —Skin that was damp and fair
> Is barklike and, feel, rough.

Gunn is determinedly cutting out his past so he can rediscover himself. He is casting out the paternal influence that hangs over him so he can 'harden/Towards a completion, mine'. The father-figure, the symbol of authority, is to be dispensed with so the poet can return to mother earth:

> I stamp upon the earth
> A message to my mother.
> And then I lower my horns.

The title poem of *Moly* owes something to Ted Hughes's 'View of a Pig' *(Lupercal)*. Hughes's pig has 'pink white eyelashes', Gunn's has 'pale-lashed eyes'. Hughes tells us that a pig's 'bite is worse than a horse's....They eat cinders, dead cats', Gunn's pig 'bites through anything, root, wire, or can'. The difference between the two poems is that Ted Hughes's pig is a dead pig. Thom Gunn's pig wants to become a man:

> From this fat dungeon I could rise to skin
> And human title, putting pig within.

> I push my big grey wet snout through the green
> Dreaming the flower I have never seen.

Gunn has changed his tune. At one time he admired animals for their uncomplicated life of instinct. Now he sees spirituality as the essence of the human being.

A note of warning against taking chemically-induced spirituality too seriously is sounded in 'The Sand Man' which begins by reminding us we are in San Francisco:

> Tourists in summer, looking at the view,
>> The Bay, the Gate, the Bridge,
> From sands that, yearly, city trucks renew,
>> Descry him at the postcard's edge.

'Him' is the Sand Man who has attained a state of innocence not through expansion of the mental faculties, but by their drastic, vicious reduction:

> After the beating, thirty-five years since,
>> A damaged consciousness
> Reduced itself to that mere innocence
>> Many have tried to repossess.

What Gunn is searching for is not 'mere innocence' but an informed innocence, an adult intellect allied to a child-like response. This is the perfect synthesis.

'Three' is about precisely 'the adult's attempt to repossess innocence, an attempt here partially successful'.[6] Gunn, expert swimmer that he is, watches three naked bathers: father, mother and three-year-old son. After their swim, as father and mother dry themselves, Gunn notices the patches of white where their bodies have been deprived of sunlight. They have been wearing bathing costumes in a moral sense as well. They lack 'the heat that sponsors all heat, from the sky'. Their son, by contrast, is unselfconsciously naked, brown all over and lost in play, and it is only by learning from their son that the parents will 'learn their nakedness'. Although the poem is based on an anecdote—what

6 *Let the Poet Choose*, ed. James Gibson, London (Harrap) 1973, p. 69.

the poet saw at the seaside—Gunn invests it with dignity. The rhythm is brisk, the rhymes weighty as waves, the imagery elemental:

> Near, eyes half-closed,
> The mother lies back on the hot round stones,
> Her weight to theirs opposed
> And pressing them as if they were earth's bones.

'From the Wave' stays by the side of the sea. Adults are attempting to return to nature, in this case to that part of nature from which man emerged: the sea. Surfers, 'black shapes on boards', are metamorphosed into 'half wave, half men'. They are able to lose themselves in the 'mindless heave' of the sea. They are able to cast off their adult inhibitions and become like children:

> They paddle in the shallows still;
> Two splash each other;
> Then all swim out to wait until
> The right waves gather.

'Three' and 'From the Wave' are linguistic models of controlled innocence, examples of the poet's ideal.

Continually aware that man has both animal lust and human intellect, Gunn tries to examine the tension involved in this apparent dichotomy in 'Tom-Dobbin' which, as the title indicates, is about a creature who is man from the waist up (intellect), beast from the waist down (instinct). In the mechanical routine of sex, Gunn argues, the mind is disengaged from the body:

> Hot in his mind, Tom watches Dobbin fuck,
> Watches, and smiles with pleasure, oh what luck.

Synthesis of mind and body comes in the act of passion and Gunn achieves this synthesis by a magnificent description of the ultimate intensity, the orgasm:

> In coming Tom and Dobbin join to one—
> Only a moment, just as it is done:

> A shock of whiteness, shooting like a star,
> In which all colours of the spectrum are.

Passion, then, comes in spasms of intensity. In the hiatus between such fusions the intellect takes over, at least in Gunn's case.

Gunn has always been good at beginning and ending his books and in *Moly* he has saved the two most lyrical and beautiful poems for the end. 'The Discovery of the Pacific' involves a very personal discovery. A couple have driven from Kansas to California in search of the sun. On their journey they sleep rough and increasingly experience a union with nature. By the time they reach the Pacific ocean—again, the sea as the element from which man evolved—they have discovered not only sunlight and sea and the elements but the exalted place human beings play in the ecology of nature. Especially human beings in love:

> Now they stand chin-deep in the sway of ocean,
> Firm West, two stringy bodies face to face,
> And come, together, in the water's motion,
> The full caught pause of their embrace.

'Come' is used here, obviously, in the sense of shared orgasm: the ultimate passion, the necessity of human creativity and renewal.

Finally: 'Sunlight'. It is beautifully lyrical, an unashamed hymn to the sun, yet the lyricism is controlled. In so perfectly synthesising passion and intellect, submission and control, the poem embodies the solution Gunn has been searching for. He acknowledges that the sun is simply a star that will die like other stars: 'its concentrated fires/Are slowly dying' as ever more and more hydrogen is converted to helium. Yet if we accept the inevitability of death we must also live intensely to compensate for the end that is to come. Gunn transfigures the explosive force that is the sun into an image of a massive sunflower in two of the finest stanzas he has written:

> Great seedbed, yellow centre of the flower,
> Flower on its own, without a root or stem,
> Giving all colour and all shape their power,
> Still re-creating in defining them,

Enable us, altering like you, to enter
Your passionless love, impartial but intense,
And kindle in acceptance round your centre,
Petals of light lost in your innocence.

That does not simply describe life as a beautiful experience: it
demonstrates it. It is light years away in expression and intention
from the work of the young man who thanked heaven for 'all
the toughs through history'. It is the work of a man who accepts
that the world is not simply a testing ground for the individual
ego but the home of a whole species capable of living together.

At the present time (August 1974) Thom Gunn has not published
a generally available collection of poetry since *Moly,* nor has he
any immediate plans to do so. He has, however, published three
limited editions—*Songbook* (1973), *To the Air* (1973), *Mandrakes*
(1974)—which will probably form at least part of his next full-
length collection.

Songbook is vintage Gunn. All the eight pieces are hard-bitten
songs sung by people down on their luck, full of self-pity and
despair.

To the Air contains five short poems and a longish five-part
sequence 'The Geysers', written in couplets of iambic pentameter.
The Geysers of the title are in Sonoma County, California. Until
recently 'you could camp there for a dollar a day'. Poem 1,
'Sleep by the Hot Stream', sets a modest mood. Gunn watches
stars from his sleeping-bag and in the morning he and his friends
'get up naked as we intend to stay'. Poem 2, 'The Cool Stream',
introduces the concept of the *ad hoc* hippie community where

People are wading up the stream all day,
People are swimming, people are at play.

The people do their own thing: 'Some rest and pass a joint,
some climb the fall'. They have come to submit to nature in
order to unite with it and with each other.

Poem 3, 'The Geyser', compares Gunn's human inadequacy
with the elemental power of the geyser, the 'searing column of
steam from ash'. However Gunn, in this sybaritic mood, recognizes
'Fire at my centre, burning since my birth/Under the pleasant

flesh'. The penultimate poem in the sequence, Poem 4, 'Discourse from the Deck', preaches a pacifist ethic. From the vantage point of space the earth seems unified. This is an illusion:

> Stop here, above America at war.
> Great varied land, of ebullience and despair,
> Too green you'd think for guilt.

Gunn's somewhat naive solution to America's ills is the model hippie society where 'a group of men loll naked, strewn/On planks that scorch in the long late afternoon'. They are privileged, of course, lucky to be alive and well and living in California, but Gunn is all for luck:

> These strangers similarly talkative,
> Generous, and joking, share the luck they live.

Gunn believes that if everyone were privileged and happy it would be possible for each person to contain the violence within him. He wants the world to be one big happy hippie community made up of people like himself:

> So many that they could at last be joined
> And cancel the self-destructiveness of the land,
> Until the America as seen down here
> Would be the same as the land you see appear
> As the globe turns, from high in outer space,
> One great brave luminous green-gold meeting place.

It's not everyone's cup of tea or joint of grass or brave new world. But in this simple vision of good intentions, making an Eden on earth, Gunn has found tranquillity. As so much of his poetry is personal, about his search for identity, this is at least the end of one search.

In the final poem of 'The Geysers'—Poem 5, 'The Bath House', which Gunn thinks 'something of a step forward, hope so anyway[7]—Gunn gives himself entirely to the warmth induced by

7 Letter, 17 March 1974.

human companionship. In a hot bath, aware of the 'sharp-sweet drifting fume of dope' Gunn surrenders his senses to his surroundings (like the child in the bath who opens *Positives*). At last he manages to lose his identity—'Not certain/who I am or where'—leaving the way open for a complete renewal at a later stage. He feels reborn, part of mother earth. He dives into a stream and shoots upward (like his goddess of energy, Proserpina, in 'The Goddess' in *Touch*). He is no longer cut off by his intellect from the warmth of others. He is 'free...I am part of all'. He has discovered what it means, being happy to be human:

> I am
> I am raw meat
>   I am a god.

Mandrakes begins, as *To the Air* ends, with

> A pure
> bold plunge into
>
> down a rope of
> bubbles.
>   ('The Plunge')

Mandrakes contains ten poems all of them written in a fluid free verse, all of them sensuous. 'Wrestling With Angels' is, according to Gunn, 'An attempt to deal with the way we acquire knowledge intuitively (as, for an example, an animal does).'[8] It tries to get 'behind words' and receive

> messages from
>   sun and moon.

The final poem of *Mandrakes,* 'Breaking Ground', shows Gunn refuting the traditional notion of death. Part 1, 'Kent', describes the death of an old woman. Gunn, born in Gravesend in Kent, finds it hard to accept the idea of the annihilation of the old woman. In part 3, 'Monterey', he resolves her death because

8 Letter, 7 October 1972.

although the body falls to the ground, and is buried in it, it is organically absorbed into future generations. So we leave Gunn on a triumphant note, exulting in the continuity of life:

It
comes to me at last that
when she dies she
loses indeed
that sweet character, loses
all self, and
is dispersed—but dispersal
means
spreading abroad:

she is not still contained
in the one person, she
is distributed
through fair warm flesh
of strangers
some have her touch, some
her eyes, some her
voice, never to be
forgotten: renewed again
and again throughout
one great garden which
is always here.

5 'In the Beginning was Scream'

While the whole gist of Thom Gunn's poetry was moving away from an egocentric projection of the self to a submission to a collective image of Eden, Ted Hughes was walking in the opposite direction. His journey has taken him nearer and nearer to an apocalyptic vision of the world. Despite the versified nightmares for children presented in *The Earth-Owl and other Moon People*, the general poetry-reading public was not really prepared for *Wodwo*. This appeared in May 1967 when Hughes was still only 36, a comparatively young man. Its overall mood was one of depression and the only humour that lurked in the book was bible-black. On the other hand, students of poetry had had an inkling of what was to come when *Recklings* appeared in a limited edition of 150 copies in 1966.

Recklings are the smallest, weakest animals in a litter, those least suited for survival. So the very title of this limited edition warns the reader not to take the poems more seriously than the author does. However, some of these recklings have been preserved. 'Logos' reappears in the British edition of *Wodwo* with minor changes ('burning pentagram' becomes 'blinding pentagram', 'Space shudders in nightmare' becomes 'Creation convulses in nightmare'); 'Public Bar TV', completely rewritten in the British and American editions of *Wodwo*, is included with three other poems (which become parts I, II and III of 'Root, Stem, Leaf' and also appear in the American edition of *Wodwo*) in the British and American editions of *Selected Poems 1957–67*.

Recklings shows a major redirection of Hughes's poetic talent. Whereas his earlier poems had been rooted in physical reality ('The Bull Moses' and 'An Otter' from *Lupercal*, for example) the tone is now surrealistic, the imagery illogical and free-associative. Even the pessimism has changed, from a personal sadness to a positive distrust of the world. There are thirty-two poems in *Recklings* and they all, with a couple of exceptions like 'Guinness' and 'Keats', discern a state of rottenness at the heart of the world.

At times the hatred verges on paranoia, as in 'Toll', with its portrayal of modern English life:

> These are the aged who hide their sadness
> And deaths in rinds of bacon and are inherited by flies;
> These are the children multiplied every morning
> With the harvest of hen-eggs; these are the suburbs
> Bearing their cargo of people under the skylines.

This is not despair but disgust. It is as if Hughes can find nothing to redeem the world—no faith, no moments of spiritual insight, nothing.

The distasteful aspect of *Recklings* is not that Hughes should have succumbed to disgust but that he should have been willing to trade in his magnificent gifts of description for nit-picking attacks on basically inoffensive physical and intellectual weaklings. Hughes sees all intellectuals as grotesquely limited and this comes over as little more than a sneering superiority complex. In 'Tutorial' books are 'Tomb-boards/Pressing the drying remains of men' while the university scholar is singled out as a murderer of writers:

> He is fat, this burst bearskin, but his mind is an electric
>   mantis
> Plucking the heads and legs off words, the homunculi.
> I am thin but I can hardly move my bulk, I go round
>   and round numbly under the ice of the North Pole.
>
> This scholar dribbling tea
> Onto his tie, straining pipe-gargle
> Through the wharfe-weed that ennobles
> The mask of his enquiry.

Nor do working men escape from Hughes's disgust. Working men ('Men that have been bending all their lives/In the one dim lamp of a pension') are drinking in 'Public Bar T.V.' They watch the television, 'That glass, bubble-bodied, dream-foetus of shadow-pallor', and what they see is man landing on the moon. According to Hughes they can no more comprehend the import of man on the moon than they can comprehend their own limitations:

> They haze and sip, like a mountain-range in the dew.
> These are the Giant Stupids.
> They are grimy to the spinal fluid
> As if they slept nightly in the earth.
>
> Mankind floats up the air in a peephole cloud—
> That's moonland!
> They can't comprehend. They undergo it like death.
> They swallow all its drizzling nothings, like the mild
>   earth.

This contempt for the man in the street is itself an intellectual arrogance of the sort Hughes is so keen to attack in other people. It is superficial, too, for a fleeting glimpse of faces in a pub tells nothing whatsoever about the individuals behind these faces. It is irresponsibly easy to sneer at everything.

Fortunately, in the version of 'Public Bar TV' that appears in *Wodwo* Hughes has wiped the sneer from his face. This time the workers in the pub vicariously identify themselves with the characters in a Western:

> Outriders have found foul water. They say nothing;
> With the cactus and the petrified tree
> Crouch numbed by a wind howling all
> Visible horizons equally empty.

This time the criticism of the mindless staring of the drinkers is couched in black humour. The arid wasteland in the Western that the watchers identify with is an image of the emptiness of their own life.

Wodwo is in three parts: Part I contains 21 poems; Part II five stories and a radio play; Part III has 19 poems. (The American edition differs in that Part I contains 22 poems—instead of 'Logos' it has 'Root, Stem, Leaf' and 'Scapegoats and Rabies'—while Part III contains only the opening section of 'Gog'). The title comes from *Sir Gawain and the Green Knight*:

> Sumwhyle wyth wormes he werres, and wyth wolves als,
> Sumwhyle wyth wodwos, that woned in the knarre.

A wodwo, is 'a sort of half-man half-animal spirit of the forest'[1] and in the concluding poem of the book, the title poem 'Wodwo', Hughes speaks as a wodwo becoming conscious of the world for the first time. Like man, the wodwo has both an animal appetite and a human brain. Like man the wodwo is uncertain of his relationship with the external world of phenomena:

> Do these weeds
> know me and name me to each other have they
> seen me before, do I fit in their world? I seem
> separate from the ground and not rooted but dropped
> out of nothing casually I've no threads
> fastening me to anything I can go anywhere
> I seem to have been given the freedom
> of this place what am I then?

That question—'what am I then?'—haunts every piece in the book and they are all meant to interrelate in a 'single adventure'

> The stories and the play in [Wodwo] may be read as
> notes, appendix and unversified episodes of the events
> behind the poems, or as chapters of a single adventure
> to which the poems are commentary and amplification.
> Either way, the verse and the prose are intended to be
> read together, as parts of a single work.[2]

And it is not only Hughes who is seeking after identity. In Wodwo the plants and the hills are all straining towards an expression of personality. The book thus elevates the pathetic fallacy (the attribution of human feelings to inanimate objects) to a poetic principle. Outcrop stone 'expects to be in at the finish' ('Still Life'); trees 'are afraid they too are momentary/Streams' ('A

---

1 Hughes, *Poetry in the Making*, London (Faber & Faber) 1967, p. 62.
2 Hughes, 'Author's Note' to *Wodwo*, p. 9.

Wind Flashes the Grass'); a hill 'suspects nothing' ('Sugar Loaf');
mountains are 'Smiling on the distance, their faces lit with the
peace' ('Mountains'); the sea is 'bored with the appearance of
heaven' ('Pibroch'). Nor is this simply a stylistic mannerism. On
the evidence of *Wodwo* Hughes apprehends a power at work in
the world, a will that works on every aspect of the world.

This will is the presence of a malevolent God, a bad artist,
a being who makes a mess out of creating the earth, a spirit that
has brought forth a planet infested with nightmare. 'Logos'
introduces this God, who 'gives the blinding pentagram of His
power/For the frail mantle of a person/To be moulded onto'.
His gift of the planet earth to frail mankind is the burnt offering
of a nightmare:

> Creation convulses in nightmare. And awaking
> Suddenly tastes the nightmare moving
> Still in its mouth
> And spits it kicking out, with a swinish cry—
>   which is God's first cry.

Hughes's pessimism is so profound that, like Schopenhauer, he
sees life as suitable only for completely destructive beings:

> The sea pulling everything to pieces
> Except its killers, alert and shapely.
> And within seconds the new-born baby is lamenting
> That it ever lived—
>   God is a good fellow, but His mother's against Him.

God, for Hughes, is not a supreme deity but a little one, a bit
like a pedantic scholar, given a corner of the universe to tinker
about with in his fumbling way. God's mother—the mother of
creation—gives him a free hand to experiment with the earth
with, Hughes assures us, ghastly results.

In 'Mayday on Holderness' in *Lupercal* Hughes had discovered
the serpent inside himself, a snaky intestine that eats away at
the Eden apprehended in childhood. In 'Reveille' in *Wodwo* he
identifies this destructive serpent as the Biblical snake that
destroyed innocence in the garden of Eden in *Genesis*. Hughes

has said 'You spend a lifetime learning how to write verse when it's been clear from your earliest days that the greatest poetry in English is in the prose of the Bible'.[3] For Hughes, the Bible, especially the Old Testament, is one of the principal source-books of his imagery.

'Reveille' gives a portrait of the serpent, 'This legless land-swimmer with a purpose', whose aim is to destroy trust and love. He is an embodiment of the force of evil. In *Genesis* 3:1 we learn that 'the serpent was more subtil than any beast of the field which the Lord God had made'. In Hughes's poem this subtlety expresses itself as a bite into innocence:

> Adam and lovely Eve
> Deep in the first dream
> Each the everlasting
> Holy One of the other
>
> Woke with cries of pain.
> Each clutched a throbbing wound—
> A sudden, cruel bite.

The serpent has triumphed, 'his coils/Had crushed all Eden's orchards'. In 'Theology' the evil serpent is shown to lie within man, it is the intestine:

> No, the serpent did not
> Seduce Eve to the apple.
> All that's simply
> Corruption of the facts.
>
> Adam ate the apple.
> Eve ate Adam.
> The serpent ate Eve.
> This is the dark intestine.

Traditionally poets have been regarded as dreamers: Hughes dreams too but he dreams nightmares. Many of the poems in *Wodwo* are transcriptions of nightmare, and at their most intense these poems are genuinely disturbing in their extraordinary

3 *London Magazine*, January 1971, p. 14.

vividness. They have their own nightmarish logic. 'Cadenza' is a lucid dream about death—surely the death of Sylvia Plath. Some of Sylvia Plath's poems have been collected under the title *Crossing the Water* and the thematic obsessions of her poetry are recalled in 'Cadenza':

> The full, bared throat of a woman walking water,
> The loaded estuary of the dead.
>
> And I am the cargo
> Of a coffin attended by swallows.
>
> And I am the water
> Bearing the coffin that will not be silent.

Whereas 'Cadenza' is an intensely private poem—though one that communicates the brittle vulnerability of the individual in unguarded moments—'Ghost Crabs' is the kind of nightmare anyone might have. It skilfully builds up a screaming sense of alien menace from a quiet opening. The first line of the poem— 'At nightfall, as the sea darkens'—seems to set the scene for a poem along the reflective lines of, say, Matthew Arnold's 'Dover Beach'. Yet night is when the face of the world turns into darkness. It is the time given over to creatures who crawl and scramble in a love of darkness, when man cannot see real objects, when his mind is invaded by dark subconscious forces. In Hughes's poem these are crabs:

> Giant crabs, under flat skulls, staring inland
> Like a packed trench of helmets.
> Ghosts, they are ghost-crabs.

And because they are ghosts they do not stop at emerging from the sea onto the beach. They invade the cities in a search for man:

> They spill inland, into the smoking purple
> Of our woods and towns—a bristling surge
> Of tall and staggering spectres
> Gliding like shocks through water.

Their presence convinces Hughes that the world is one long prolonged nightmare. For 'these crabs own this world', 'They are the powers of this world', 'They are the turmoil of history', 'They are God's only toys'.

In *The Hawk in the Rain* and *Lupercal* Hughes was able to turn to animals for their inbuilt impulse, their functional clarity, their lack of 'indolent procrastinations and...yawning stares'. Not in *Wodwo*. Now the animals have become symbolic, unreal. The symbols are made that much more powerful because they are welded to an utterly convincing physical appearance. Take 'Second Glance at a Jaguar'. In talking about the poem Hughes no longer regards the jaguar simply as an animal, but as symbolically much more:

> the more concrete and electrically charged and fully operational the symbol, the more powerfully it works on any mind that meets it....A jaguar after all can be received in several different aspects...he is a beautiful, powerful nature spirit, he is a homicidal maniac, he is a supercharged piece of cosmic machinery, he is a symbol of man's baser nature shoved down into the id and growing cannibal murderous with deprivation, he is an ancient symbol of Dionysus since he is a leopard raised to the ninth power, he is a precise historical symbol to the bloody-minded Aztecs and so on. Or he is simply a demon...a lump of ectoplasm. A lump of astral energy.[4]

Hughes has come a long way—some would say regressed—since 'The Jaguar' in *The Hawk in the Rain*, the animal that won't be caged. He has stepped inside the cage and entered the spirit of the animal in 'Second Glance at a Jaguar'. And if the above description of the poem makes it sound more like that of a fortune-teller than a poet then it is just as well that Hughes's best poems can speak for themselves. For once he is inside the cage the subject takes over. The poem is a catalogue of simile and metaphor in which the animal is defined by his assumption of roles he seems temperamentally suited for. Hughes gets under the skin of the

4 *Ibid*, pp. 8–9.

jaguar. Metaphorically the animal is 'Skinfull of bowls' and 'Gangster, club-tail lumped along behind gracelessly'. In the similes he is 'Like a cat going along under thrown stones'; has a 'terrible, stump-legged waddle/Like a thick Aztec disembowel-ler'; has a 'belly like a butterfly'; has a head 'like the worn down stump of another whole jaguar'; in movement is 'Going like a prayer-wheel'. The jaguar is a criminal, 'Muttering some mantrah, some drum-song of murder' while his coat bears 'rosettes, the cain-brands'. Finally, the poem puns on 'underworld' as both the jungle the jaguar comes from and the criminal underworld:

> He coils, he flourishes
> The blackjack tail as if looking for a target,
> Hurrying through the underworld, soundless.

The same symbolic charge is found in the other animal poems. 'The Bear' symbolises inertia being transformed into conscious-ness. The rat in 'Song of a Rat' is a symbol of the suffering in the universe. When it understands. as opposed to simply registering. its suffering it dies. But suffering does not die with it for the stars—the illuminations of the universe—are 'Forcing the rat's head down into godhead'. At the end of the poem the rat has become the deity of suffering. 'The Howling of Wolves' makes wolves symbols of pain, at the mercy of 'the steel traps' and crying like a baby 'you cannot say whether out of agony or joy'.

There is one spark of joy in *Wodwo*, otherwise all is dark. The light relief comes in 'Full Moon and Little Frieda', a poem for the poet's daughter. Frieda Rebecca. born 1 April 1960 in the London flat rented by Hughes and Sylvia Plath. Shortly after the birth of Frieda they bought the thatched house in Devon which is the setting of the poem. Instead of the poet's terrified response to the 'wide eyeball' of the moon in 'New Moon in January' we have the child's innocent, delighted reaction to the dead world that circles the earth. In 'A cool small evening shrunk to a dog bark and the clank of a bucket' the child is astonished at the moon and can only try to capture it by naming it repeti-tively:

> 'Moon' you cry suddenly, 'Moon! Moon!'

> The moon has stepped back like an artist gazing amazed
> at a work
> That points at him amazed.

For a moment Hughes is able to share that innocence, just long enough to transcribe it.

However, the solitary highlight only further emphasises the darkness around, and parts of *Wodwo* are very dark. 'The Rescue', a poem bristling with metaphorical muscle, is a nihilistic account of the worthlessness of our civilisation, a civilisation sustaining only death and despair instead of life. The poem is a narrative account of a vivid nightmare. Five people are stranded on an island. Into their world comes a ship 'the white bow-wave/ Cleaving the nightmare, slicing it open,/Letting in reality'. And what a reality: the sailors on the ship are 'white/As maggots'. As the boat comes to pick up the five survivors Hughes considers the possibility of a romantic rescue

> When the rowboat's bows bit into the beach
> And the lovely greetings and chatter scattered.

But just as we are thinking that Hughes has suddenly become enamoured of the idea of man-made civilisation he says:

> This is wrong.
>   The five never moved.
> They just stood sucked empty
> As grasses by this island's silence.

On the journey back to the ship 'The five sat all the time/Like mummies with their bandages lifted off'. This suggests that they have died one death in shared isolation on the island but also that their resurrection, their rescue, is about as valid as the Egyptian belief in the resurrection of mummified bodies.

'Stations' contemplates the death of the old. In part I an old man succumbs to death, loses his 'drowsy mind' while his widow clings to the debris that remains of him: a tulip, his jacket, his last pillow. Hughes describes death as the most relevant fact of life:

Whether you say it, think it, know it
Or not, it happens, it happens, as
Over rails over
The neck the wheels leave
The head with its vocabulary useless,
Among the flogged plantains.

'The Green Wolf', thematically linked to 'Stations', describes the effects of a stroke, causing a man to lose the power of half his body:

the left hand seems to freeze,
And the left leg with its crude plumbing
And the left jaw and left eyelid and the words, all the
huge cries

Frozen in his brain his tongue cannot unfreeze.

Far from moving Hughes to compassion this merely makes him contemplate the rubbishy wastage of old age: 'One smouldering annihilation/Of old brains, old bowels, old bodies'.

Hughes's poetry has a deep pessimism linked to his fascination with war, particularly World War One. *The Hawk in the Rain* had six poems about war. *Wodwo* has 'Scapegoats and Rabies' (in the American edition), 'Bowled Over'—about a soldier's 'Desertion in the face of a bullet!'—and 'Out'. Hughes absorbed his knowledge of World War One at the feet of his father who saw action in Gallipoli. When I visited Bill in July 1974 in his house in Heptonstall Slack he began to talk about the war. He began by shaking his head and saying 'it were a rough do' and went on to produce his Smallbook which had been so packed with Yorkshire mementoes that it had stopped a piece of shrapnel from entering his body. In the first part of 'Out' Hughes remembers this and reveals that it was his infant imaginary participation in World War One, via his father's stories, that destroyed the Eden of childhood:

My father sat in his chair recovering
From the four-year mastication by gunfire and mud,...

> While I, small and four,
> Lay on the carpet as his luckless double,
> His memory's buried, immovable anchor,
> Among jawbones and blown-off boots, tree-stumps,
>   shell-cases and craters,
> Under rain that goes on drumming its rods....

The second part of 'Out' tells, proleptically, of the birth of a dead man. It is an image of a generation of children born for a precise function: to die. It is also the birth of a child such as Hughes for whom innocence is impossible because of the consciousness of death. Such a birth Hughes compares to a 're-assembled infantryman' who is blasted to bits, then

> Tentatively totters out, gazing around with the eyes
> Of an exhausted clerk.

The final part of the poem takes up the image of the birth of death a bit further. For the poppy is 'the mouth/Of the grave, maybe of the womb searching'. Hughes feels cheated by the war's destruction of his childhood, for World War One not only buffeted his father but clung on to the four-year-old Hughes

> Holding my juvenile neck bowed to the dunkings of the
>   Atlantic.
> So goodbye to that bloody-minded flower.

The phrase recalls the title of Robert Graves's World War One autobiography *Goodbye to all That*. Hughes wants an end to the worship of death, he desperately wants to say 'Goodbye to the cenotaphs of my mother's breasts./Goodbye to all the remaindered charms of my father's survival'.

Other poems in *Wodwo* relentlessly deal in death. If man is to be judged by his actions—and by calling a poem 'Karma' Hughes endorses this Buddhist viewpoint—then man is grotesque. Hughes finds man guilty of a multitude of sins: Dresden, Buchenwald, the Irish atrocities, the mass-extermination of Jews—to name a few. These things, too, he blames for the impossibility of innocence, for his own opportunities of innocence 'have melted like my childhood under earth's motherly curve'. In 'Ballad from a Fairy Tale' he has a glimpse of the childhood innocence that eluded him in the horror stories of war and on the depressing rainsodden Pennine moors. He sees, as in a dream, 'a swan the size of a city' then realises 'it was no swan/It was a white angel'. It is a symbol of innocence that cannot survive in the valleys of Hughes's youth, for

> this enormous beauty
> Passed under the rough hilltop
> Opposite the house
> Where my father was born
> Where my grandmother died.
> It passed from my sight.
> And the valley was dark.
> And it had been a vision.
> That was long ago.

Innocence, this suggests, will forever elude him.

Finally: 'Heptonstall'. As the local guidebook says 'The ancient village of Heptonstall sits proudly and secure on the steep hillside above Hebden Bridge, boasting a history richer and more fascinating than most other Pennine settlements'.[5] It has the oldest continually-used Methodist church in the world, it was ravaged by the Great Plague in 1631, John Wesley preached there. Ted Hughes's father was centre half for the Hebden Bridge Association Football Club and, after running a shop in Mytholmroyd (where Ted was born), returned to live in his present house. There is a fifteenth-century church tower and a nineteenth-century church in Heptonstall and, according to local tradition, the graveyard round the two churches holds the remains of 100,000 bodies. On 18 February 1963 Sylvia Plath was buried in this graveyard. There is a simple stone commemorating her with the words:

> Even amidst fierce flames
> The golden lotus can be planted.

5 Philip Round, *Heptonstall History Trail*, West Riding (Calder Civic Trust) 1973.

For Hughes it is not simply a village any more but the symbolic centre of his pessimistic universe. A mound of decaying death:

> Black village of gravestones.
> The hill's collapsed skull
> Whose dreams die back
> Where they were born.

He concedes that 'Life tries' and 'Death tries' and 'The stone tries' but everywhere there are the ubiquitous tears of a despairing heaven raining down, for 'Only the rain never tires'.

The middle section of *Wodwo* is prose, five stories and a radio play. All the stories are nightmarish transcripts of dreams. Each story has an element of menace in it: the horse in 'The Rain Horse', the blizzard in 'Snow', the rats in 'Sunday', the tractor in 'Harvesting'. Above all, the natural elements are omnipresently oppressive, reflecting Hughes's obsession with the physical life-force of the country. The title-poem of *The Hawk in the Rain* began with the image of ploughland sucking man back into itself. In 'The Rain Horse' the same image recurs:

> The ankle-deep clay dragged at him. Every stride was a
> separate, deliberate effort, forcing him up and out of the
> sucking earth, burdened as he was by his sogged clothes
> and load of stone and limbs that seemed themselves to
> be turning to mud.

This passage in itself indicates the fierce life that Hughes sees in nature, a life that man ignores at his own peril. Man is rooted in nature and loses his function when he becomes deracinated by moving to cities.

The man in 'The Rain Horse' is such a deracinated man, a countryman who has lost his roots in the country. After twelve years' absence he comes back to a valley of his childhood. However, nature is not ready to accept him:

> Twelve years had changed him. This land no longer
> recognised him, and he looked back at it coldly, as at a
> finally visited home-country, known only through the

stories of a grandfather; felt nothing but the dullness of feeling nothing.

As if taking revenge on this deserter of nature, nature sends a symbol of her power. First rain, then a 'thin, black horse' which runs 'like a cat, like a dog up to no good' and looks 'like a nightmarish leopard'. The horse is after the man. It pursues him, physically attacks him, putting him in a state of impotent terror. But then something happens. The man changes. He loses his civilized manners and becomes animal-like himself, reacting to the danger by retaliating with stones. He has returned to his primitive element. He has recovered his animal instinct:

> He looked around for stones. The encounter had set the
> blood beating in his head and given him a savage
> energy. He could have killed the horse at that moment.
> That this brute should pick him and play with him in
> this malevolent fashion was more than he could bear.
> Whoever owned it, he thought, deserved to have its
> neck broken for letting the dangerous thing loose.

Its neck broken, notice: the man has returned to a state where forces, not individuals, confront each other. After the man has driven the horse away he recuperates in a shed, remembering his roots, remembering 'three dead foxes hanging in a row from one of the beams, their teeth bloody'. The man turned animal has gained an instinct but lost his lust for civilisation, for he 'just sat staring at the ground, as if some important part had been cut out of his brain'. It had: his debilitating intellect, his civilised habit of 'indolent procrastinations'. The only real difference between the stories and the poems in *Wodwo* is that Hughes follows the rules of clear narrative and logical development in the stories. The nightmares are the same.

'Sunday' reads very much like an autobiographical reminiscence of Hughes's childhood. For it begins with a boy, bored by chapel sermons, retreating into an imaginative world:

> Finally he closed his eyes and began to imagine a wolf
> galloping through snow-filled, moonlit forest. Without

fail this image was the first thing in his mind whenever he shut his eyes on these situations of constraint, in school, in waiting-rooms, with visitors. The wolf urged itself with all its strength through a land empty of everything but trees and snow.

The boy is called Michael and he feels his whole world overcast by the fact that it is Sunday: 'There was even something Sundayish about the pavements, something untouchably proper'. Michael wants something stronger, a sight of the legendary Billy Red the rat-catcher who performs every Sunday, twelve on the dot, in the Top Wharf Pub. Billy's appearance is startling: 'Scarecrowish, tawny to colourless, exhausted, this was Billy Red, the rat-catcher'. It is not long before his adversaries make their appearance: 'Hunched in opposite corners of the cage, their heads low and drawn in and their backs pressed to the wires so that the glossy black-tipped hairs bristled out, were two big brown rats'. The ritual that follows is described with horrific relish. First the rats are pinned by their tails to the bottom of the cage. Then Billy bites the first rat to death. Horrified by the naked confrontation between man and beast Michael leaves before Billy Red finishes off the second rat. The story, complementary to 'Song of a Rat' where the creature is a symbol of suffering, leaves one with more sympathy for the rat than for Billy Red.

However unpleasant 'Sunday' is, it is a nightmare of reality. Such things happen, or Hughes persuades us that this is so. 'Snow', however, is nightmare as pure as the driven snow that permeates the obsessive narrative which, unlike 'The Rain Horse' and 'Sunday', is first-person. The survivor of an air disaster reckons he has been walking through an endless blizzard for five months. He is thus totally at the mercy of hostile elements, pitted against nature at her most remorseless. His only weapon is his intellect. And it is only a key to madness. The man has a chair which he uses to fight off his fear of solipsism, in a vain attempt to gather evidence 'of a reality beyond my own'. He gives his meaningless life meaning by playing a game with the chair, almost losing it in the process. It is an allegory of intellectual life, a death-in-life that turns on itself:

But my chair is here, on my back, here. There's no danger of my ever losing it. Never so long as I keep control, keep my mind firm. All the facts are on my side. I have nothing to do but endure.

From the cold of 'Snow' we move to the 'unnatural heat' of 'The Harvesting'. This story involves metamorphosis. Mr Grooby has come during the harvesting to hunt hares. The weather swelters and while he lies still waiting for the hare, the tractor and cutter tackle the wheat, and out-of-work colliers (doubtless of the type described in 'Her Husband') help with the harvesting. Mr Grooby endures the intolerable heat for three hours. It affects him so much that reality appears to dissolve into dream in front of him. Seeing a hare he shoots but the kickback of the gun knocks him unconscious. He begins to become a hare. It is a nightmare: 'His sense cleared a little and as at the moment of waking from nightmare to the pillow and the familiar room, Grooby realised he was lying face downward in the wheat'. His nightmare is of being cut up by the 'mincer' (the same nightmare that appears in the poem 'Sunstroke' in *Lupercal*). By the time he is ready for a second shot at the hare he has empathised with it. He can see, as if in a mirror, the hare's features, 'the roughness of its brindled, gingery flanks and the delicate lines of its thin face'. He watches it charge up the hill to safety and becomes himself the hare:

> The dogs were behind him with their inane yapping. He began to shout at them and shouted louder than ever when he heard the sound that twisted from his throat, the unearthly thin scream. The enormous white dog's head opened beside him, and he felt as if he had been picked up and flung and lost awareness of everything save the vague, pummelling sensations far off in the blankness and silence of his body.

'Suitor' is the weakest of the tales. A young man has come to see his girl only to find a rival waiting for her, a rival who is dismissed by a second rival. The latter ends up watching the narrator obsessively and playing the flute. There is no powerful narrative as in the other four stories, only an impression of the narrator's nervous, hypersensitive inability to distinguish between appearance and reality. But the other four stories show Hughes with a sound narrative sense and a capacity for evoking nightmares in the everyday world. The radio play 'The Wound'—broadcast by the BBC Third Programme on 1 February 1962—tells of the near-insanity of Ripley, a soldier with a bad headwound, as he walks nine miles through hallucination. In his fantasy his dead comrades live again but it is nothing but illusion. Whether Hughes will go much further in the field of imaginative prose and drama remains to be seen. Meanwhile it is his poetry that concerns us.

Crow, an expressionist sequence of poems, was published in October 1970 and by April 1974 Faber & Faber had sold more than 20,000 copies of the book. That is remarkably good going for a book of poetry, and especially for one that is so unrelentingly macabre. It offers no edification, it resolves no weighty questions, it just keeps on crowing at the creation. The book began when Leonard Baskin the American sculptor suggested Hughes should write a series of texts to accompany engravings. The resulting book was to be published by Baskin's Gehenna Press. Both Hughes and Sylvia Plath admired Baskin's work enormously and in her book *The Colossus* Sylvia Plath has a poem, 'Sculptor', dedicated to Baskin as a latter-day Pygmalion. What Hughes intended was an epic folk-tale alternating prose and verse. What he has published, however, is the verse.

The first edition of *Crow* contained 59 poems. It was reprinted twice in 1970 and twice in 1971 and a new edition in 1972 contained seven new poems: 'Crow Hears Fate Knock on the Door', 'Crow's Fall', 'The Contender', 'Crow Tries the Media', 'Crow's Elephant Totem Song', 'Crowcolour', 'Crow Paints Himself into a Chinese Mural'. All these poems, with the exception of 'Crowcolour', appear in the American edition of *Crow* which has 'The Lovepet' in place of 'Crowcolour'.

Hughes has made several statements on *Crow*. In an interview with Egbert Faas he said:

> The idea was originally just to write his songs, the songs that a Crow would sing. In other words, songs with no music whatsoever, in a super-simple and a super-ugly

language which would in a way shed everything except just what he wanted to say without any other consideration and that's the basis of the style of the whole thing. I get near it in a few poems. There I really begin to get what I was after.[6]

In a letter to me he said:

> One of the starting points was that the Crow, as the bird of Bran, is the oldest and highest totem creature of Britain. Bran's oracular head was buried in Tower Hill, saying that England could not fall while he stayed there, but Arthur—it is said—dug it up, because he wanted England to be defended by his strength alone. But the birds were kept. During the last war the ancient lineage of ravens at the Tower died out and new ones had to be brought in, and their wings clipped to keep them there. The crow was also Odin's bird—therefore the totemic bird in chief of the Angles, Saxons, etc., and of the Norsemen. England pretends to the lion—but that is a late fake import. England's autochthonous Totem is the Crow. Whatever colour of Englishman you scratch you come to some sort of Crow.[7]

And in a radio interview he said:

> The main story takes the Crow through a series of experiences which alter him in one way and another, take him to the bottom and then take him to the top, and eventually the whole purpose of the thing is to try to turn him into a man, which the story, as it stands, nearly succeeds in doing. . . .[8]

Earlier in the last interview, when Hughes was asked 'if you've written about crows before at all?' he answered: 'No'. This

6 *London Magazine*, January 1971, p. 20.
7 Letter, 27 February 1973.
8 'Poetry Now' broadcast on BBC Third Programme, 24 June 1970.

assertion is repeated in a monograph on Hughes where we are told that 'up to 1963 Hughes had never written about crows'.[9] It is not strictly accurate. In 'Griefs for Dead Soldier' in the *Hawk in the Rain* (1957) corpses are buried while 'Under the blue sky heavy crow and black fly move'. This conforms to the tradition of associating the crow with death. In 'Mayday on Holderness' in *Lupercal* (1960) death lives with the fact that 'The crow sleeps glutted and the stoat begins'. In 'November', also from *Lupercal*, death is again linked to the crow:

> The keeper's gibbet had owls and hawks
> By the neck, weasels, a gang of cats, crows.

A third *Lupercal* poem 'Snowdrop', dwelt on the murderous power of nature where

> Weasel and crow, as if moulded in brass,
> Move through an outer darkness
> Not in their right minds,
> With the other deaths.

So for Hughes the crow has always been a symbolic bird, an image of destruction. In a play written in 1964 (though not published until 1971 and then only a limited edition of 150 copies), *Eat Crow*, the connexion between death and the predatory bird is made explicit. Morgan, a confused Everyman, is interrogated by a cunning Prosecution and in a search for his own identity enters a dream world more real than the everyday world. He conducts a choir of women, he referees a mob, he becomes the centre of attraction. Then the play closes with a dialogue between Morgan and She in which they consider the similarities between a crow and 'a man, lying alone, among stones, with a rifle, lying limply, in a waterless land, in a grey desert of tumbled stone, with one bullet, a man dryer than a lizard'. The play closes:

9 Keith Sagar, *Ted Hughes*, Harlow, Essex (Longman for the British Council) 1972, p. 27.

SHE: The crow is composed of terrible black voice. He is neither stone nor light. But voice that can hardly utter. He looks this way and that. The forms of the stones, the fractures of heavenly accident, the resolute quality of light, hold the crow anaesthetised, every hour more skilled in patience, resigned to the superior stamina of the empty horizon, limber and watchful.

MORGAN: The laws are still with the living.

SHE: The crow arrived before dawn, smelling the man, and settling to watch at extreme range.

MORGAN: And when he saw the crow, in the blue thinning light, the man gave thanks to the studded baleful pallor of the heavens, and to this strange-faced company of stones. His prayer has produced hot quails and not manna. A crow has come up from the maker of the world.

SHE: The crow watches the man.

Hughes's Crow is such a powerful symbol of malicious destructiveness because the symbol is so rooted in the facts of the life of a real crow. The crow inhabits the whole earth apart from Antarctica. It is cunning, feeding on putrid flesh, and will eat afterbirth or attack ewes in labour, pecking out their eyes. It is the most intelligent of the birds and uses its intelligence to exploit the weak and helpless. In Hughes's poetic sequence Crow represents the mistakes that God has made. Crow is God's nightmare, a mistake that can talk back and crow over the mess that is humanity, the failure of the Garden of Eden. And the nightmare is more potent than the dream.

Crow is Ted Hughes's *Genesis*. Where the Biblical *Genesis* at least offers a Paradise to return to, Hughes's *Genesis* does not accept that there was ever any hope for man. He was born to be eaten away by the serpent inside him. The Biblical *Genesis* begins

> In the beginning God created the heaven and the earth.
> And the earth was without form, and void; and
> darkness was upon the face of the deep....
> And God said, Let there be light: and there was light.

119

Hughes challenges this account of the beginning in 'Lineage':

> In the beginning was Scream
> Who begat Blood
> Who begat Eye
> Who begat Fear
> Who begat Wing
> Who begat Bone

and so on until we come to Adam

> Who begat Mary
> Who begat God
> Who begat Nothing
> Who begat Never
> Never Never Never
>
> Who begat Crow.

So the end-product of all creation is Crow who comes 'Screaming for Blood/Grubs, crusts/Anything'.

Crow gets a passport into the world in 'Examination at the Womb-Door' on the principle of the survival of the cruellest. Because Crow has 'scrawny little feet', 'bristly scorched-looking face', 'unspeakable guts', 'wicked little tongue' and so on, he is 'stronger than death'. Which is an enviable strength, for in God's world

> Who owns the whole rainy, stony earth? *Death.*
> Who owns all of space? *Death.*

Crow is born for survival: in 'A Kill' he emerges from the womb of space as a monster of blood and bone and guts and is greeted with the cry 'It's a boy' before everything goes black. Crow's mother is deep space which is also the mother of God (remember 'Logos' in *Wodwo*: 'God's a good fellow but His mother's against him'). Like his mother, Crow is black. But Crow is the joint creation of God and deep space and from God he has inherited unpleasant characteristics as we see in 'Crow and Mama'. When he cries he burns his mother's ears; his laughter makes his mother weep; his attempts at walking scar her face; his tantrums wound her. Yet Crow has an Oedipus complex: basically he loves the black emptiness of his mother, and hates God his father. So when he reaches for the stars he falls flat on his face on the menstrual moon and 'crawled out/Under his mother's buttocks'. However, he has made a discovery and 'The Door' tells what that discovery is. The creatures on earth are weighed down by a grave guilt:

> All are rooted in earth, or eat earth, earthy,
> Thickening the wall.

The wall is life. And Crow finds 'a doorway in the wall—/A black doorway:/The eye's pupil'. His appearance, he feels, will penetrate the wall.

In 'A Childish Prank' Crow invents sex. God has created Adam and Eve and falls asleep pondering on the problem of what to do with them. Enter Crow. Crow bites 'the Worm, God's only son' into two:

> He stuffed into man the tail half
> With the wounded end hanging out.

> He stuffed the head half headfirst into woman
> And it crept in deeper and up
> To peer out through her eyes
> Calling its tail-half to join up quickly, quickly
> Because O it was painful.

Thus Crow spoils God's creation of man and woman. He reduces them to creatures who can never know love, only the vile urge to join the two ends of the internal serpent together. While God sleeps, Crow laughs. This poem is a brilliant piece of black comedy and typifies the whole tone of *Crow*. It is a book in which solemnity is energised into laughter.

Having seen the results of Crow's invention of sex God attempts to teach his filial adversary the concept of love in 'Crow's First Lesson'. When Crow tries to say the word 'Love' nature vomits with repulsion. Crow can only conceive of hate so his croaks destroy the idea of love. First man's 'bodiless prodigious head' sprouts on the earth while 'woman's vulva dropped over man's neck and tightened'. At this obscene spectacle Crow flies away guiltily. He knows he brings out the worst in man by playing on his innate fear of sex, his Oedipus complex. Even Crow sees the hell that is in man and woman and, in 'Crow Alights', he 'shivered with the horror of Creation'. Determined to oppose God's handiwork—knowing that 'Nothing escaped him. (Nothing could escape.)'—he wishes for the nightmare to fade: 'He blinked. Nothing faded.' The nightmare has become permanent. If Crow is to make the worst of a bad job then he 'had to start searching for something to eat' ('That Moment').

Crow, in 'Crow Tyrannosaurus', feels that creatures are the sum of what they eat: 'The swift's body... Pulsating/With insects', 'the dog was a bulging filterbag/Of all the deaths it had gulped', 'Even man he was a walking/Abattoir/Of innocents—/His brain incinerating their outcry'. Crow considers stopping this consumption of life by setting a spiritual example—'ought I/To stop eating/And try to become the light?'—when he succumbs, like the others, to his appetite:

> But his eye saw a grub. And his head, trapsprung,
> stabbed.
> And he listened
> And he heard
> Weeping.

The weeping is the agony of existence. For man exists in a perpetual battlefield. And he has the capacity intellectually to contain suffering, to abstract it from agony, to normalise it. This becomes clear in 'Crow's Account of the Battle', a 'terrific battle', a battle that 'had happened too often before/And was going to happen too often in future'. In a brilliant reversal of his hitherto hyperbolic images Hughes, speaking for Crow, shows how man can come to accept murder as part of the daily round:

> And shooting somebody through the midriff
> Was too like striking a match
> Too like potting a snooker ball
> Too like tearing up a bill
> Blasting the whole world to bits

> Was too like slamming a door
> Too like dropping in a chair
> Exhausted with rage.

Man's ability to rationalise everything eventually takes death out of killing, makes a mannerism of murder.

A crow is a black beast, a traditional *bete noir*. In 'The Black Beast' Crow tries to find the root of evil unaware that it is lodged inside him. He denies the black beast, splits his enemy's skull, crucifies a frog under a microscope, peers into the brain of a dogfish. In doing these things he becomes the black beast and more and more like a man with every line that passes. Man, from this viewpoint, has nothing to smile about and in 'A Grin' happiness cannot find a home in the world. A 'hidden grin' searches for somewhere to settle. It concentrates on people with no apprehension of happiness, tries to help them: it seeks out a woman in childbirth, a man in a car-crash, a machine-gunner, a steeplejack crashing to his death, two lovers. But there is no happiness. Even the man in the electric chair rejects the grin which then disappears knowing it is a misfit, knowing there is no room for it on earth.

In 'Crow Communes' God is asleep again, exhausted with Creation, taking a Sunday nap after his week's work. Crow takes a bite out of God's shoulder and finds a foul taste in his mouth. God, it seems, is as rotten as the world he has created. Even the saints are monstrous. 'Crow's Account of St George' implies that the battle against evil only creates further evil. The patron saint of England becomes the dragon he is trying to kill. For the evil is within him and cannot be exorcised. Nor do words do anything but define this internal evil. 'A Disaster' shows the murderous impact of words on man. They make him acutely aware of evil but unable to combat it. The animal in Crow can resist words:

> Words attacked him with the glottal bomb—
> He wasn't listening.
> ('The Battle of Osfrontalis')

Man, being human, is at the mercy of words. And this, too, is a mistake for God, in Hughes's fable, does not speak like a man:

'God spoke Crow' ('Crow's Theology'). And just as God dissociates himself from man, Crow dissociates himself from other birds in 'Crow and the Birds'. The eagle, curlew, swallow, swift, owl, sparrow, heron, bluetit, woodpecker, peewit, bullfinch, goldfinch, wryneck, dipper—they all remain in a world of their own. Crow is too intelligent to be a mere bird. Crow cannot stop poking his beak in man's rubbish: 'Crow spraddled head-down in the beach-garbage, guzzling a dropped ice-cream'. Crow interferes in the world of man because he has so much in common with the murderous aspect of man, whose dreams die in the face of the fact of blood:

> And when he began to shout to defend his hearing
> And shake his vision to splinters
> His hands covered with blood suddenly.
> ('Criminal Ballad')

For even if we reject the mythical origin of man, the biologists and evolutionists trace him back to the sea, which is a murderous element. 'Crow on the Beach' ponders this Godless theory of man's emergence from 'the sea's ogreish outcry and convulsion'.

As the sea is the mother of man, space is the mother of Crow. This only intensifies Crow's Oedipus complex. In 'Oedipus Crow' our hero's insides sicken at the thought of his mother's indifference and his father's incompetence, at nightmarish visions of mothers that become 'Mummies...With their bandages and embalming honey'. In this nightmare Crow doesn't have a leg to stand on, loses his roots, and is comforted only by the passing of time measured in the thump of his one foot, in the tick of a watch. Time, though, is the voice of Death.

> So Death tripped him easy
> And held him up with a laugh, only just alive.

It is a warning against Crow's vanity. Crow is losing his animal instinct and becoming more like a man.

In 1967 Ted Hughes adapted Seneca's *Oedipus* for production by Peter Brook at the National Theatre. In 'Song for a Phallus' Hughes gives Crow a chance to have a go at the story. As Crow's attempt to murder God the father is the dynamic of so much of Crow it is natural that 'Song for a Phallus' should be central to the book. Crow knows his Freud. He knows that, according to the Oedipus Complex, all boys go through a phallic stage of sexual desire for the mother and corresponding hatred of the father they fear will castrate them:

> O do not chop his winkle off
>   His Mammy cried with horror
> Think of the joy will come of it
>   Tomorrer and tomorrer
>   Mamma Mamma.

The refrain 'Mamma Mamma' is a childish cry of desire and despair. The way Crow tells the story Oedipus attempts matricide as well as patricide because the mother is ultimately responsible for the horror of existence:

> He split his Mammy like a melon
>   He was drenched with gore
> He found himself curled up inside
>   As if he had never been bore
>   Mamma Mamma.

This cyclical poem draws an additional meaning from its context in the *Crow* sequence. For, seeing that it is the serpent of evil that curls up inside human beings, Oedipus the murderer incestuously enters his mother like a phallic snake.

In 'Apple Tragedy' it is the mother of all men, Eve, who is sexually penetrated by the serpent, and at her own bidding:

> Eve drank and opened her legs
>
> And called to the cockeyed serpent
> And gave him a wild time.
> God ran and told Adam
> Who in drunken rage tried to hang himself in the
>   orchard.

They are both under the influence of drink, which is only a temporary release from rationality. Adam tries to kill the serpent out of jealousy, Eve claims it was all a case of rape. Neither will acknowledge the evil that dwells inside them.

From now on, as Hughes says in 'Apple Tragedy', 'everything goes to hell'. In 'Crow's Last Stand' the sun begins to expand in an attempt to destroy the earth. Crow survives. In 'Crow and the Sea' it is water's turn to be 'bigger than death' but Crow survives. He 'marched away from the sea'. In 'Truth Kills Everybody' Crow seeks out the amphibian Proteus to see if he can master the sea. Crow tries to murder Proteus who undergoes a series of metamorphoses: becoming Achilles, a shark, a naked powerline, a screeching woman, Christ's heart. All this knowledge unsettles Crow whose grip becomes so neurotically tight that 'He was blasted to nothing'. But he does not die. Instead, in 'Crow and Stone', 'Crow has become a monster'. He needs to be in a world that is dying as 'the sun comes closer, growing by the minute' ('Notes for a Little Play'). For man has learned how to make his own sun, the hydrogen bomb, and he is stupid enough to believe that the existence of love in the world will prevent a nuclear holocaust:

> Nothing else has happened.
> The love that cannot die
> Sheds the million faces
> And skin of agony.
>
> ('Snake Hymn')

But there is no love. There is only man and woman trying to destroy each other. There is only the satisfaction of the two halves of the serpent sliced by Crow in 'A Childish Prank'. This becomes—to use the closing phrase from 'Two Eskimo Songs'—'utterly clear' in 'Lovesong'. The lovers tear each other to pieces, an example of man's inability to love humanity:

> His words were occupying armies
> Her laughs were an assassin's attempts
> His looks were bullets daggers of revenge

Her glances were ghosts in the corner with horrible
   secrets
His whispers were whips and jackboots.

Only Crow can survive the holocaust because, having seen man
in action, he finally gives up humanity as a dead loss and reverts
to his predatory nature in 'King of Carrion'. Crow's 'palace is
of skulls', and his 'crown is the last splinters/Of the vessel of life'.
But man has destroyed himself so Crow's triumph is empty, an
endless watch over a destroyed world. In this 'empty world' all
Crow can do is 'To reign over silence'. Hughes closes the sequence
with Crow's hollow triumph. He has learned the nature of man
but it is a destructive knowledge. We leave Crow

> Grown so wise grown so terrible
> Sucking death's mouldy tits.
>   ('Littleblood')

I have deliberately concentrated on isolating the fable that
emerges from *Crow* because it is the overall impact of this, rather
than that of individual sections, that contains the power of the
book. Like the Biblical sources from which it is drawn, *Crow* is
repetitive. But this does not weaken the book, rather it allows
for an accumulation of imagery. The style, which is consciously
unsubtle and bludgeoning, is suitable for the revelation of the
apocalypse which engulfs mankind in *Crow*. It is a British book
of the dead, a long hard, bloodthirsty look at the meaning of
the myths we blandly put in the bookshelves along with the
Bible. It is Hughes's most impressive sustained performance to
date and shows him as a poet with the talent to trade in new myths
for old.

It is impossible to predict exactly where Hughes is going as a
poet. Certainly the naturalism of *The Hawk in the Rain* and *Lupercal*
did not suggest a poet of massive powers of myth-making, which
is what Hughes has become in *Crow*. Subsequent events suggest
that he is in a transitional stage (as he was in the years following
the death of Sylvia Plath when he chose to publish books for
children and pursue his adult poetry in private). In 1971, the
year following the publication of *Crow*, Hughes participated in
an extraordinary experiment. Commissioned by Peter Brook's

International Centre for Theatre Research Hughes invented an original organic language. Using the Prometheus myth Hughes evolved a language that was so rooted in physical phenomena that he believed it could break through the international communication barrier and impart a deep, archetypal meaning to all peoples regardless of the language they spoke. The play that Hughes wrote, *Orghast,* was performed at Persepolis.

The title of *Orghast* comes from two words invented by Hughes (though his inventions are based on the onomatopoeic theory of the origin of language): ORG, life; GHAST, spirit. This passage, spoken by God-Krogon, is an evocation of Creation. Hughes's intention is that the language should make an emotional rather than a cerebral impact and it is up to each reader to test this personally by reading the passage aloud. Hughes's translation is printed beneath the *Orghast* text:

BULLORGA OMBOLOM FROR
darkness opens its womb

SHARSAYA NULBULDA BRARG
I hear chaos rear

IN OMBOLOM BULLORGA
in the womb of darkness

FREEASTAV OMBOLOM
freeze her womb

NILD US GLITTALUGH
rivets like stars

ASTA BEORBITTA
icy chains

CLID OSTIA BULLORGA
lock up the mouth of
darkness

IN OMBOLOM KHERN FIGYA
    GRUORD.
in her womb I make my words
    iron.

Since then Hughes has written a series of poems beginning, like 'A Bedtime Story' in *Crow* and as many of Vasco Popa's poems do, 'Once upon a time there was a person'. These poems certainly suggest that Hughes is involved in further exploration of the possibilities of narrative verse. In fact, his latest publication, *Spring Summer Autumn Winter*—which appeared in a limited edition of 140 copies in June 1974 and in a general edition entitled *Season Songs* in 1976—is a series of narrations of the seasons primarily intended for children. They show that his intense involvement in the mythical *Crow* sequence has done nothing to weaken Hughes's magnificent gifts of observation. In addition, the poems are rooted in the reality of nature so that children will know what it is all about—a struggle, not a picture-postcard existence. For example 'A March Calf' reminds us, just as we are enjoying the look of 'this dear little fellow' (the calf) that

> Hungry people are getting hungrier,
> Butchers developing expertise and markets.

And in 'Spring Nature Notes' there is a note of menace when Hughes insists to his readers, apropos of the rays round an oak tree: 'They disturb you', while 'Sheep' maintains that 'The woe of sheep is like a battlefield/In the evening, when fighting is over'.

One of the finest poems, 'Swifts', shows that even if one act of kindness cannot alter the cruelty of nature, there is still a point in caring:

> Every year a first-fling nearly-flying
> Misfit flopped in our yard,
> Groggily somersaulting to get airborne.
> He bat-crawled on his tiny useless feet, tangling his
>   flails,
>
> Like a broken toy, and shrieking thinly
> Till I tossed him up—then suddenly he flowed away
>   under
> His bowed shoulders of enormous swimming power,
> Slid away along levels wobbling
>
> On the fine wire they have reduced life to,
> And crashed among the raspberries.
> Then followed fiery hospital hours
> In a kitchen. The moustached goblin savage
>
> Nested in a scarf. The bright blank
> Blind, like an angel, to my meat-crumbs and flies.
> Eyelids resting. Wasted clingers curled.
> The inevitable balsa death.

Finally burial
For the husk
Of my little Apollo—

The charred scream
Folded in its huge power.

6   'Thinking too precisely'

After the previous chapters it is fair to say: Ted Gunn is dead,
long live Thom Gunn and Ted Hughes. Two poets who live
thousands of miles apart, who have totally different lifestyles and
aspirations, who have never been inseparable friends or colleagues,
cannot be considered as two ways of looking at the same thing.
And though as poets they are still in mid-stride, the direction of
their work differs: Gunn has undergone a journey from anxiety
to ecstasy. Hughes has increasingly immersed himself among the
dark powers he believes control the world. Gunn is renewing
a tradition that means so much to poetry, and he offers his own
striking personality as the content of his poetry. Hughes is an
original in his poems of direct observation, and in his best work
he is a man possessed by poetry.

Yet to me the greatest disappointment in Gunn and Hughes
is the way they have failed to respond to the revolutionary potential
of twentieth-century society, have been unable to see the epic
significance of our scientific age. Instead they live within themselves, they look back to the past, they see cultural decay. Such
attitudes spring from an inability to find in life the excitement
and interest they have found in books. T.S. Eliot had the same
limitation and wrote *The Waste Land* to contrast the squalid
present against the magnificence of dead literature. It is only
the university attitude it is not the truth. The truth of our society
is that man cannot live by books alone. It is an escape from
responsibility to affect contempt for poetry while exclusively
living the life of a poet. It is selfish to view the search for one's
own identity as the most important fact of life—only those with
a privileged environment can even begin to think like this and
that excludes the majority. Poetry, if it is to survive, must surely
move from its aristocratic stance to a democratic insistence that
poetry is not elitist but the most memorable way of saying things

that matter. Gunn and Hughes have so much talent at their disposal that time will tell if they are capable of taking the plunge into reality. Meanwhile their work remains impressive but too often only if we accept the poet as a man apart from real life. How long can he continue to be? That is the question.

Select Bibliography

1 Poetry by Thom Gunn

Poems. Fantasy Poets, No. 16, Oxford (Oxford University Poetry
Society) 1953.

Fighting Terms, Swinford (Fantasy Press) 1954; revised New York
(Hawk's Well Press) 1958; re-revised, London (Faber &
Faber) 1962.

The Sense of Movement, London (Faber & Faber) 1957; Chicago
(University of Chicago Press) 1959.

My Sad Captains, London (Faber & Faber) 1961; Chicago (University of Chicago Press) 1961.

Positives, London (Faber & Faber) 1966; Chicago (University of
Chicago Press) 1966.

Touch, London (Faber & Faber) 1967; Chicago (University of
Chicago Press) 1967.

Poems 1950–1966: A Selection, London (Faber & Faber) 1969.

Sunlight, New York (Albondocani Press) 1969. Limited edition
of 176 copies.

Moly, London (Faber & Faber) 1971; *Moly and My Sad Captains,*
New York (Farrar, Straus & Giroux) 1973.

Songbook, New York (Albondocani Press) 1973. Limited edition
of 226 copies.

To the Air, Boston (David R. Godine) 1973. Limited edition of
200 copies.

Mandrakes, London (Rainbow Press) 1974. Limited edition of
150 copies.

2 Poetry by Ted Hughes

The Hawk in the Rain, London (Faber & Faber) 1957; New York
(Harper & Brothers) 1957.

Lupercal, London (Faber & Faber) 1960; New York (Harper & Brothers) 1960.

Meet My Folks! London (Faber & Faber) 1961; New York (Bobbs-Merrill) 1973. For children.

The Earth-Owl and other Moon-People, London (Faber & Faber) 1963; extended as *Moon Whales*, New York (Viking Press) 1975. For children.

Nessie the Mannerless Monster, London (Faber & Faber) 1964; New York (Bobbs-Merrill) 1974. For children.

Scapegoats and Rabies, London (Poet & Printer) 1965. Limited edition of 400 copies. The text of this sequence appears in the American edition of *Wodwo* and in *Selected Poems 1957–1967*.

Recklings, London (Turret Books) 1966. Limited edition of 150 copies.

The Burning of the Brothel, London (Turret Books) 1966. Limited edition of 300 copies.

Wodwo, London (Faber & Faber) 1967; New York (Harper & Row) 1967.

Five Autumn Songs for Children's Voices, Bow, Devon (Richard Gilbertson) 1968. Limited edition of 500 copies.

Crow, London (Faber & Faber) 1970; New York (Harper & Row) 1971; new edition with seven additional poems, London (Faber & Faber) 1972; limited edition of 400 with three additional poems and twelve drawings by Leonard Baskin, London (Faber & Faber) 1973.

Selected Poems 1957–1967, London (Faber & Faber) 1972; New York (Harper & Row) 1974.

Spring Summer Autumn Winter, London (Rainbow Press) 1974 (limited edition of 140 copies); published as *Season Songs*, London (Faber & Faber) 1976.

3 By Thom Gunn and Ted Hughes

Selected Poems, London (Faber & Faber) 1962. Contains selections from Gunn's *Fighting Terms*, *The Sense of Movement* and *My Sad Captains;* and from Hughes's *The Hawk in the Rain* and *Lupercal*.

Five American Poets (ed.), London (Faber & Faber) 1963. Selections from Edgar Bowers, Howard Nemerov, Hyam Plutzik, Louis Simpson, William Stafford.

4 Other books by Thom Gunn

Poetry from Cambridge 1951–1952 (ed.), London (Fortune Press) 1952.

Selected Poems of Fulke Greville (ed.), London (Faber & Faber) 1968; Chicago (University of Chicago Press) 1968.

Ben Jonson (ed.), Harmondsworth, Middlesex (Penguin) 1974.

5 Other books by Ted Hughes

Here Today (ed.), London (Hutchinson) 1963. School anthology.

How the Whale Became, London (Faber & Faber) 1963; New York (Atheneum) 1964. Prose for children.

Selected Poems of Keith Douglas (ed.), London (Faber & Faber) 1964; New York (Chilmark Press) 1964.

Poetry in the Making, London (Faber & Faber) 1967; as *Poetry Is,* New York (Doubleday) 1970. Text of radio anthology for schools.

The Iron Man, London (Faber & Faber) 1968; as *The Iron Giant,* New York (Harper & Row) 1968.

A Choice of Shakespeare's Verse (ed.), London (Faber & Faber) 1968.

Seneca's Oedipus, London (Faber & Faber) 1969; New York (Doubleday) 1972. Adaptation of David Turner's translation from the Latin.

The Coming of the Kings and other plays, London (Faber & Faber) 1970, as *The Tiger's Bones,* New York (Viking Press) 1973. Radio plays for children.

Eat Crow, London (Rainbow Press) 1971. Limited edition of 150 copies.

A Choice of Shakespeare's Verse (ed.), London (Faber & Faber) 1971.

The Story of Vasco, London (Oxford University Press) 1974. Adaptation of George Schehadé's *L'Histoire de Vasco* as libretto for Gordon Crosse's opera.

6 Criticism

DODSWORTH, M. (ed.): *The Survival of Poetry,* London (Faber & Faber) 1970, pp. 133–63 ('Ted Hughes' by Derwent May) and pp. 193–215 ('Thom Gunn: Poetry as Action and Submission' by Martin Dodsworth).

FAAS, E.: Interview with Ted Hughes in *London Magazine,* n.s., Vol. 10, No. 10, Jan. 1971, pp. 5–20.

GRUBB, F.: *A Vision of Reality,* London (Chatto & Windus) 1965, pp. 203–13 ('Peacetime Conscript: Thom Gunn') and pp. 214–25 ('Thinking Animal: Ted Hughes').

HAMILTON, I.: Interview with Thom Gunn in *London Magazine,* n.s., Vol. 4, No. 8, Nov. 1964, pp. 64–70.

——*A Poetry Chronicle,* London (Faber & Faber) 1973, pp. 165–70 (reprint of his 8 January 1971 *TLS* review of *Crow*).

HOLBROOK, D.: 'The Cult of Hughes and Gunn' in *The Poetry Review,* Summer 1963, pp. 167–83.

MANDER, J.: *The Writer and Commitment,* London (Secker & Warburg) 1961, pp. 153–78 ('The Poetry of Thom Gunn').

PRESS, J.: *Rule and Energy,* London (Oxford University Press) 1963, pp. 181–91 (on Ted Hughes) and pp. 191–201 (on Thom Gunn).

RABAN, J.: *The Society of the Poem,* London (Harrap) 1971, pp. 165–71 (on *Crow*).

ROSENTHAL, M.L.: *The New Poets,* New York (Oxford University Press) 1967, pp. 224–33 ('Ted Hughes') and pp. 251–7 ('Thom Gunn').

SAGAR, K.: *Ted Hughes,* Harlow, Essex (Longman for the British Council) 1972.

——*The Art of Ted Hughes,* London (Cambridge University Press) 1975.

SMITH, A.C.H.: *Orghast and Persepolis,* London (Eyre Methuen) 1972 (on Ted Hughes's participation in the creation of *Orghast*).